WHY ME LORD?

Advice from a
successful failure

D0531112

MICHAEL
APICHELLA

**kevin
mayhew**

WHY ME, LORD?

ADVICE FROM A SUCCESSFUL FAILURE

MICHAEL APICHELLA

First published in 2002 by
KEVIN MAYHEW LTD
Buxhall, Stowmarket, Suffolk IP14 3BW
E-mail: info@kevinmayhewltd.com

9 8 7 6 5 4 3 2 1 0

ISBN 1 84003 902 7
Catalogue No 1500501

Cover design by Angela Selfe
Edited and typeset by Elisabeth Bates

Printed and bound in Great Britain

Contents

About the author

Michael Apichella, 48, grew up in North America. An award-winning journalist, he is a university lecturer, a lay preacher and a conference speaker. A former BBC radio producer, Michael now contributes regularly to the *New Christian Herald*, *Woman Alive*, the *Catholic Life* and other periodicals. He is the author of *The Church's Hidden Asset* (Kevin Mayhew, 2001) and co-author of *Prisoner of Hope*, written with former UDA terrorist Billy McFetridge (New Wine, 1998). He and his family have made England their home since 1985. Although he has known many setbacks in his personal and professional life, he says failure has been his greatest teacher.

This book is dedicated to Albert and Elisabeth Taylor, who gave friendship to me when I needed it most, and to Mike and Anita Pepper, who practise what they preach.

Foreword

It has been said that God does not see you as a failure; he sees you as a learner. Yet there are so many books on the market, including the Christian market, that tell us how to succeed, always be good at, ever victorious. We are confronted with the 'prosperity' gospel, and the view that being successful is the indispensable sign of God's blessing and our spirituality. There is also the cult of the successful. People write books because they have a success story to tell; and you too can be successful if you follow their simple neat formula.

We live in Christian circles where we are encouraged to be winners, on top, with no problems, difficulties or weaknesses. When we meet together as Christians we always feel we have to put on a brave front and hide our dark, weak spots because we Christians are always meant to have everything together all the time and be on top. But life is just not like that. When we are honest and truthful we all know we have areas of weakness and failure and disappointments. This is true of our human experience – it is true of biblical experience.

I am so pleased that Michael Apichella has written this honest, down-to-earth, thoroughly biblical book, that deals with life as it is for Christians, warts and all. He himself is no stranger to disappointment and failure.

In his book Mike honestly explores the experiences and disappointments that we all meet at some time. He encourages us to see that this is a normal part of Christian experience and growth. He shows us what the Scriptures teach about such experiences, why they happen and how we can use them, learn from them to follow Jesus more closely.

He makes excellent use of the flesh-and-blood failures of the Bible – like Moses and Peter, and of stories from famous people – like Mother Teresa and C. S. Lewis, and ordinary people who have struggled with failure and disappointment. He also openly shares his own experiences.

This is a very relevant book for this self-centred hedonistic west of ours where Christians, too, want ease and comfort and success without any effort or pain.

Mike gets us to look at what the Scriptures say to help us to make sense of the failures and disappointments that we meet and to grow more into the likeness of Jesus through these hard times. He strikes a wonderful biblical balance for these days of how to be successful.

Failure is here to stay. This book helps us understand what failure is all about, why we meet failure and how as Christians we can fail successfully, that is be learners, disciples of Jesus. As Mike often says, 'God has not called us to be successful; he's called us to be faithful.'

JIM GIRDWOOD

Introduction

Be honest. Have you ever been angry because you felt abandoned by God when you needed him the most? Do you get depressed because others seem to succeed while you just muddle along? Maybe there are times when you contemplate giving up because you feel you've made a mess of your life. If so, then this book is for you. It's about overcoming the anger, the pain, and the suffering that comes when we fail.

I've had to face plenty of failure over the years. That's why I've written a book about it. Looking back, though, some of my worst failures seem pretty funny to me now.

For instance, I once had a lead in a play. There were two lines in the script that were nearly identical. One was in the middle of Act Two and the other was late in the final act. During a matinee performance, I accidentally spoke the line from the final act during Act Two. A character from the final act who was paying more attention to a cute female stage crewmember than to the play heard his cue and strolled out on stage and blurted out his lines. The other actors and I made round eyes and said nothing for a full second (an eternity on stage!) Reluctantly, we responded with our final-act lines, bringing the play to a confused early ending. That was the beginning of the end of my acting career.

I'm a failed carpenter, too. During a period of unemployment, I heard about a job on a building site. Following a brief interview, the boss casually asked me if I could read blueprints. I said I could. 'The job's yours,' he said. 'Start helping those men over there.'

An hour later, while I was sawing a length of wood, the boss startled me by shoving a blueprint at me and announcing to the crew, 'Mike's in charge.' He told me what he wanted built and said he'd be back in the morning to check the work. When the boss came back, he wanted to wring my neck. All of my calculations were exactly $1/4$-inch out. Everything had to be torn down and started over, and I was promptly demoted.

Despite having won awards for my radio work, I have also made some award-winning blunders on the air. During the Bosnian war, for instance, I was presenting a news bulletin on a London radio station. Suddenly fresh information about a battle rolled onto my screen. As I read it, I became panicky when I spotted a polysyllabic place name in the last sentence. Taking a bite of air, I charged forward and tripped over the pronunciation. Clearing my throat, I tried the name again with no success. When I tried for the third time to say the name, I opened my mouth but no words would come. My fast-thinking co-presenter opened his mic and pronounced the name perfectly and ended the bulletin for me. As I came off air, I had to run the gauntlet of colleagues and staff who ragged me about my gaffe.

Other failures are not so funny. My wedding day, for example, ended in disaster. Even though I was in love, I called off the wedding. My breach of promise forced my fiancée to explain the situation to baffled guests, and her parents were stuck with a huge bill for a wedding reception that never happened.

We all have painful and lonely experiences, but they need not destroy us.

I hope this book will be a tool of encouragement to Christians who, like me, have been wounded – whether through poverty, a broken marriage, humiliation, failing health, an ineffectual ministry, unemployment, bad choices, or any of a hundred other possible torments. In the pages ahead, I want to show that no matter how seriously we fail, we shouldn't give up.

Curiously, failure is sometimes necessary before we can succeed. For instance, Walt Disney went broke several times and had a nervous breakdown before he became a household name. Opera supremo Enrico Caruso failed so many times with his high notes that one voice teacher advised him to give up. He didn't. Instead, he persevered and became one of the world's greatest tenors. Albert Einstein and rocket scientist Werner von Braun both failed courses in maths. Henry Ford was financially bankrupt when he was 40. Thomas Edison's schoolteacher called him a dunce, and later he failed over 6,000 times before he perfected the first electric light bulb.[1]

The Bible has more than its fair share of failed saints, too. Trainee missionary John Mark was savagely criticised by the apostle Paul because the young man had let him down during an important mission outreach in Pamphylia. This led to a quarrel and a long-term rift between Paul and fellow missionary Barnabas. Can you imagine how badly all three saints must have felt? (Acts 15:36-41).

What about you? Have you ever failed when you set out to serve God? For better or worse, we've been conditioned to judge ourselves by our achievements. And when our achievements don't match up to our expectations, the results can be withering.

But there is hope. For one thing, failures don't destroy

us. In fact, they may teach us valuable lessons that make our faith stronger. Failed missionary John Mark, for instance, appears to have survived his humiliation and continued with his calling. The result? Ten years later, Paul wrote a glowing report of John Mark's abilities (2 Timothy 4:11).

In the pages ahead, we'll look at the lives of many biblical and contemporary men and women. All have known crushing defeats, but their lives prove the truth of Romans 8:28: 'We know that in everything God works for good with those who love him, who are called according to his purpose'.

Chapters 1-5 of this book describe five specific reasons why I believe God allows us to fail. Chapter 6 focuses on the paradox of Christian failure, our need to rejoice and praise in times of trouble, and how to find hope when our outlook is bleak. Chapters 7-11 deal with the nature, the consequences, and ultimately, the benefits of occasional personal defeat by examining the lives of two of the Bible's best-known failures, Moses and Peter. Chapters 12-14 show that often we must fail before we can discern God's will for our lives. The Epilogue offers practical advice for using your failures to help any that are discouraged by various setbacks.

Incidentally, I don't pretend to know every reason why God allows Christians to fail. No one may claim to know that. It is a futile exercise to manipulate events to fit in with our own finite understanding of the infinite mind of the Lord. When we question God with our limited human understanding, as Job tried to do, God's staggering response always must be, 'Who is this that questions my wisdom with such ignorant words?' (Job 38:2, NLT). Job, placed in checkmate by the logic of God's reply, wisely speaks a word of faith, 'I know that you can do anything, and no one can stop you' (42:2). Job's example teaches us that ultimately the Christian life is one of faith – faith that even in agonising and confusing situations, God is with us; therefore, we may trust him in every situation, good or bad.

Although the two are closely linked, this book is about failure, not suffering *per se*. In every case, what I have to say is applicable to individual, not corporate failure. Therefore, I do not address such topics as earthquakes, the World Trade Centre atrocity, or the plight of the starving millions in the world. My purpose is to shed light on the reasons why we fail, offering a way forward when the foundations of our lives feel like they are crumbling beneath our feet.

Finally, when people are trying to make sense of their failures, there is a tendency to reject the encouragement of the written word. That's when support from other Christians is invaluable. By reading this book, perhaps you can be used to help someone to catch hold of hope.

1. From 'Failure never forever', Dick Innes, www.gospelcom.net. Quoted with permission.

CHAPTER ONE

Keeping us humble
and dependent on God

Mother Teresa of Calcutta made things happen. Following her first appearance on BBC television, viewers sent thousands of pounds to the broadcasting company to support her Christian work. Yet no appeal for money had been made. While visiting her in India, the Pope gave her his white ceremonial automobile as a gift. After he returned to the Vatican, the enterprising nun raffled it off to the highest bidder, raising enough money to open her first leper mission. Whenever members of the *glitterati* visited Mother Teresa, they invariably donated money to help her in her work.

When Mother Teresa announced that she would open a mission in London, it was generally thought that such a project would take months, if not years, to establish. It was up and running in two weeks.

It would take a book twice the size of this one to do justice to the marvellous work done by this joyful servant of God. Yet few realise that Mother Teresa went through dark periods in her life thinking that she was a failure. Evidence of this surfaced in her personal diaries. Excerpts from 1946 to just before her death in 1997 appeared in the March 2001 issue of *Vidyajyoti* (Light of Knowledge), a journal published in New Delhi by the Jesuit order.

Convinced as a young woman that God had called her to work among the poorest of the poor in India, she founded the Missionaries of Charity. By all accounts, hers was a successful ministry. However, in her own eyes, her efforts fell far short of the gargantuan task set before her. Her words reveal the pain, the loneliness and the sense of abandonment she felt at key moments in her life. She admits that in these black times she couldn't even pray. At one point, she was tempted to abandon the project and limp home to Europe in defeat. Was this what the psalmist had in mind when he wrote of a believer?

> He is like a tree planted by streams of water, that yields its fruit in its season, and its leaf does not wither. In all that he does, he prospers. (Psalm 1:3)

If we understand the psalmist correctly, failure is something reserved for the wicked, the scheming, the morally bankrupt, and other assorted 'selfish people' – not the likes of Mother Theresa. When Christians set out to serve God, surely our lives should be exempt from embarrassing failures and heartbreaking disappointments! Thus we dedicate our lives to his service knowing that he will give us only the best in this life. But what happens when Christians set about serving God in earnest, only to have their plans go wrong? What is the effect when believers feel defeated by overwhelming circumstances? Is the psalmist lying when he promises that God will not allow his people to fail?

Mother Teresa is not the only well-known Christian who lived with a profound sense of failure. After his surprising conversion out of atheism in 1930, C. S. Lewis wrote *The Great Divorce, Mere Christianity, Screwtape Letters,* and *Miracles,* books that present the Christian faith in ways that appeal to atheists and agnostics. Indeed, the 8 September

1947 issue of *Time* magazine dubbed Lewis the 'Apostle to the Sceptics' in recognition of his accomplishments. Even Lewis' fantasy series, *The Chronicles of Narnia*, written in the 1950s and which has sold over 65 million copies, is credited with bringing children and their parents to faith in Christ. Yet Lewis knew great failure.

In 1951, after 27 years of teaching at Oxford University, and making lasting contributions to the study of the English language through his academic research, Lewis was passed over for a much-deserved promotion to full professor. His elder brother, Warren, alleged that many of his brother's colleagues had voted against Lewis because of a profound anti-Christian prejudice. Warren recorded this injustice in his diary on Thursday, 8 February 1951. Lewis biographers William Griffin, Roger Lancelyn Green, Lyle Dorsett and others concur with the elder Lewis' assessment.

In 1954, in recognition of his brilliance, Cambridge University offered C. S. Lewis the Chair of Medieval and Renaissance Literature. Ever loyal to Oxford, Lewis was reluctant to accept. Ultimately, he decided it was better to go where he was wanted, and so he left Oxford never having risen higher than a lowly tutor. Derek Brewer, a former student and close friend, quotes Lewis as saying the move to Cambridge at age 56 meant that for the first time in his academic career, Lewis could ask himself each morning what he'd like to do rather than face the daily grind of tutorials.

Sadly, this richness was to be short-lived. Soon after his promotion, his American wife, Joy Davidman, contracted terminal cancer and died a slow and excruciating death. By 1961, Lewis' own health was in serious decline, eventually forcing him to resign from Cambridge and retire to the Kilns in Oxford where he died on the afternoon of Friday, 22 November 1963.

A popular misconception

Regardless of how bad our circumstances are, we must never forget that God is merciful and, above all, he is loving. In fact, his nature constantly expresses his love for his creation.

King David wrote more poetry about God's wonderful love for us than any other writer in western civilisation. Yet David was a man well acquainted with failure. When the prophet Samuel told Jesse that his son David was to be Israel's new king, the old man should have been proud of David. On the contrary. He rudely declares, 'Our David? He's hopeless. The best he can do is to muck out the sheep pens – and even that's beyond his talent!' (See 1 Samuel 16:11.) Not long after, Eliab, David's eldest brother, scolds David in public for offering to fight the Philistine giant Goliath. 'You little twerp,' said Eliab. 'Get home where you belong!' (See 1 Samuel 17:28-30.) After David killed the giant, he should have been recognised by the king as a national hero. Instead, King Saul sets about making David's life a living nightmare (Samuel 18:6-9).

David knew scores of other failures, too. Yet he knew that a loving relationship with God was worth more than success in the eyes of his contemporaries, what has come to be known as the 'good life'. Since this was so, David chose to praise God despite his frequent hard circumstances: 'Because thy steadfast love is better than life, my lips will praise thee' (Psalm 63:3). Perhaps like David, all the important people in your life consider you a failure. Maybe you set out to do some great thing for God, only to have everything go wrong. Perhaps you have been wrongly accused of some misdeed. What should we think when this happens? First, know that Christians aren't always successful. Having faith in God is not the same as taking out a cosmic insurance policy that guarantees we will never fail. This insurance policy mentality most likely comes from picking and choosing bits of scripture as we would chocolates, taking the verses we like, but rejecting the less palatable ones.

A better way to understand our failures is to study the entire Bible. There are plenty of scriptures that counter-balance so-called success verses. For example, Psalm 1 may be better understood when we read Psalm 34 which I quote in part:

> When the righteous cry for help, the Lord hears, and delivers them out of all their troubles.
>
> The Lord is near to the broken-hearted, and saves the crushed in spirit.
>
> Many are the afflictions of the righteous; but the Lord delivers him out of them all. (17-18)

Note the reference to suffering and pain: When the *righteous* cry for help; many are the afflictions of the *righteous*. Who are the righteous? They are the people of faith – you and me. Despite being 'planted by streams of water that yields its fruit in its season', Christians may expect to taste failure. However, we may rejoice in knowing that God does not abandon us when we fail; actually, he is closest to us in our suffering: 'The Lord is near to the broken-hearted, and saves the crushed in spirit. He delivers him out of them all.' So when we fail, it does not mean that we have lost favour with God.

Failure is a good teacher

Constant success is unrealistic, yet we live in a society that teaches us that being a winner isn't everything; it's the *only* thing. A well-known politician summed up his secret of success this way: 'Never admit to any wrongdoing, and reinvent yourself every four years.' The idea is to hide your failures, and talk about your accomplishments, even if you have to invent some. When it comes to this philosophy, even Christians are guilty. I have a professor friend whom I'll call Bill. After a dramatic conversion to Christianity, he left his post at a secular university to teach at a well-known theological college. Shortly after he was hired, Bill's department head invited him to lunch. Over coffee, his new boss casually enquired, 'So, tell me, Bill, how did you become a Christian?'

Bill began to talk about his life, which included a good deal of personal failure. He described a torrid love affair that he had had which led to the breakdown of his marriage and that of the woman with whom he was involved. Bill added that he suffered from acute alcoholism and depression. 'I ended my story by admitting that after finding myself in my car on the edge of a cemetery badly hungover and unable to account for how I had got there after a weekend of boozing, I knew I needed help. That's when Christ came into my life.' According to Bill, when he finished telling his story, his boss replied tersely, 'Let me give you a piece of advice, friend. Don't *ever* repeat that story to anyone around here.'

Today Bill is a fine professor, an excellent husband and father, and sober because of – not in spite of – his past failures. People like Bill know that failure is a good teacher. Jayne Ozanne, a member of the Archbishops' Council for the Church of England agrees. According to Jayne:

> How often do we see the phrase 'candidates should have nothing in their past that would cause embarrassment'?

Whilst it is of course important to be discerning over who we appoint to positions of responsibility, I believe we must be careful that we do not operate a deselection process that screens out those who have experienced God's saving grace. The Church needs leaders who have learnt the fundamental importance of repentance – and those who have been able to learn from their mistakes . . . these . . . men who ultimately feared God more than they feared men, who were open about their failings – using them as doorways into areas of greater blessings.[1]

If Christians refuse to admit to their failures and thereby learn from them, then they are destined to repeat them again and again. Moreover, if they believe that they are above failure, then the next fantasy they'll believe is the so-called prosperity gospel, the view that 'if I honour God then he'll bless me with good health, a good job, a bigger home, and a fatter bank account.' While I believe that God intends for his people to have these things and more in this life, we must not lose sight of the fact Jesus himself had no means of support, no home, not even a tomb of his own at the end of his life (Luke 9:58).

The way to succeed is to fail

To be sure, the Christian life is not an endless cycle of failure and misery. Indeed, I have seen books that are little more than pessimistic tracts concluding that misery is normal, even good, for us Christians stranded on this side of paradise. Nothing could be further from the truth. The Christian life is a successful life. Nevertheless, we must come to terms with the unpleasant side of following Jesus.

Parents know their children are destined to fail from time to time. They know, too, that with each new error, there is pain followed by growth. Failure enables children to learn from experience, to develop critical skills, which allow them to achieve their potential. Although it may be unpleasant, failure is as important as success if we hope to grow in faith and wisdom.

Let's assume that a fair amount of failure is a necessary part of life for all that call God their father. Since God is a good father, we may trust that from his perspective, our failures have the potential to bring about some success in the long run. Let's take a look at C. S. Lewis again. His colleague J. R. R. Tolkien believed that Lewis was the most brilliant scholar at Oxford of his time. Lewis knew about his gifting early on and candidly admitted that before his conversion to Christianity, he was an annoying prig. Significantly, even after his conversation experience, he struggled with the sin of intellectual pride. All of us hear about famous people who become too puffed up with themselves because of too much success. Lewis might have become an insufferable know-it-all if he had enjoyed universal approval. But because he remained a lowly don for the best part of his career while his friends eased into choice academic posts, Lewis became a humble man.

I have met people who knew Lewis personally – biographers, former students and his neighbours – and all have told me that despite his brilliance, one of the most remarkable things about Lewis was his kindness. Even though he was disappointed by the unfair treatment he received at Oxford, he did not allow it to embitter him.

A compassionate man, few of his close friends could understand why Lewis continued to look after a hot-tempered elderly friend, Mrs Moore, who never thanked him for his help. An honourable man, he nursed his brother Warren through illness and depression, encouraging him, and affirming him by welcoming him into his close circle of writer friends known as the Inklings. (Warren was a talented writer in his own right.) A generous man, Lewis quietly gave away large sums of money to needy people here and abroad. When fellow Inkling Charles Williams died, Lewis produced a book of essays dedicated to Mrs Williams and quietly saw to it that the royalties went to her.

Lewis was a jolly man. The Clark family were Lewis' neighbours in the 1950s. 'I was a boy when we moved here,' Roger Clark told me. 'And I sent Christmas cards to all our new neighbours, but only C. S. Lewis bothered to write back. Later, he invited me to visit him,' Roger added. 'That was typical of Lewis,' said Diane, Roger's mother. 'He was personable, and a joy to know.' Although his failures were painful,[2] they taught him to be more like Christ.

Consider Mother Teresa. Malcolm Muggeridge told a story about a time when he was in a car in Bengal and his driver ran into a pedestrian. Wanting to do the right thing by the poor fellow (who was not seriously hurt as it turned out), Muggeridge brought the man into the car and ordered the driver to go to the nearest hospital.

The hospital, more like a human butcher's shop, was packed to capacity with maimed and diseased human beings. With each passing second, Muggeridge's English sensibilities were shocked, until at last, a man whose throat had been cleanly slit from earlobe to earlobe, was set at their feet with his vacant eyes staring at the ceiling. This was too much. Muggeridge bolted out of the offensive hospital. On his way out, he said, Mother Theresa – a woman brimming with God's love – was cheerfully on her way in, and unlike him, she stayed and loved these poor people!

How did Mother Teresa find such love for the unlovely? I think it was precisely her own acute sense of failure that enabled her to come alongside the rejected, the diseased, and the failed masses of India.

And let's not forget St Paul, another highly gifted servant of God. Paul was ambitious and intellectual – a classic Type A personality. Even after his conversion on the Damascus Road, he remained a highly driven man. God knew he needed to teach Paul to be less self-sufficient. In 2 Corinthians 12:7, Paul confesses that God accomplished this through something called a 'thorn in the flesh'. Although no one knows exactly what Paul's torn was, it was probably some personal or physical failing on Paul's part. Paul writes:

> And to keep me from being too elated by the abundance of revelations, a thorn was given me in the flesh, a messenger of Satan, to harass me, to keep me from being too elated. Three times I besought the Lord about this, that it should leave me; but he said to me, 'My grace is sufficient for you, for my power is made perfect in weakness.' I will all the more gladly boast of my weaknesses, that the power of Christ may rest upon me. For the sake of Christ, then, I am content with weaknesses, insults, hardships, persecutions, and calamities; for when I am weak, then I am strong (2 Corinthians 12:7-12).

Notice how Paul advises us to accept our weaknesses and failures for the sake of Christ, who will see us through our pain (Luke 9:23).

Are you trying too hard?

Our culture encourages us to be ambitious. Sometimes this ambition sets us up for even greater failure. I have first-hand experience with this phenomenon. While living in the United States in February 1978, I came under the conviction that I was to be a missionary and committed my life to overseas missionary work.

To prepare, I readjusted my busy schedule in order to attend an evening Bible College. Eventually, I applied to a mission board that focused on Mexico. I was invited to an interview in Washington DC. I felt the meetings had gone well, so when I received a rejection letter a few weeks later, I was hurt and confused. The mission board felt that I needed more training, including practical experience.

Undaunted by the rebuff, I decided to seek out the right experience. In 1979, I became the youth worker at my church. This opened opportunities for me to teach, preach and help run Christian basics courses. Several months later, I again applied to be a missionary. To my delight, I had been selected by a mission outreach in Ireland.

Next, I began the task of raising my support. My church gave me a substantial grant to pay for air fare, and soon my picture and news of my plans were published in local newspapers.

It was a busy time in my life: I was teaching full-time by day, doing youth work in the evenings, and helping run the Sunday school. In between all this, I managed to run four miles each evening. Consequently, when I found myself getting occasional severe stomach pains, I ignored them.

The attacks became so bad that I finally went to see a doctor while visiting my mother in the next state. To make a long story short, on the very day my flight was to take me to Ireland, I was in a town miles from home having major surgery. Because I was out of town, everyone assumed I had gone to Ireland. Eventually word got out that I was in hospital and would be off my feet for an indefinite amount of time.

When I returned home, gaunt and using a cane, I had to begin the complicated task of returning all the money I had received from my church. Most of the deacons were understanding, but a number of people felt that I had let the side down somehow, especially the sending mission who unceremoniously dropped me from their active list and never made any effort to discover how I had fared following my hospitalisation. This both shocked and saddened me.

That was a very low point in my life emotionally and physically, and the back-to-back failure of my mission career along with my failed health made me cynical. I wrote in my journal on 27 July 1979: 'I am going to take a sabbatical from churches and Christianity.' And I did just that. I dropped out of all Christian service for the next four years. This decision turned out to be a good one. I had to learn that I was setting myself up for failure by trying too hard. Mainly, I think I was trying to imitate other so-called successful Christians I had known or had read about.

Alfred Perna, a career missionary and an Assemblies of God minister quotes the late Dr Bob Pierce, 'Don't ask God to bless what you are doing, but do what God is blessing.' There are four things that God *always* blesses:
1. God always blesses what he initiates.
2. God always blesses what depends on him (not our efforts).
3. God always blesses what is done according to his Word.
4. God always blesses what is done for his glory.

I wish I had known that 25 years ago. Ironically, I now see that my keen desire to serve as a missionary was interfering with my personal relationship with God, and this became a spiritual Achilles' heel for me. God had to allow me to fail in order to get me to focus on what *he* actually wanted me to do.

I now know doing *nothing* for God out of obedience is

better than serving him out of a sense of *ambition* – no matter how commendable that ambition may be. This is an important message of *The Practice of the Presence of God*, written by Brother Lawrence, the sixteenth-century monk. He explains that failure may come about as the result of trying too hard to please God.[3]

In reality, God simply wants to be our companion. He wants us quietly to enjoy him. Moreover, he wants us to be totally dependent on him. Only when we are able to do this, can we respond when he calls us to a task – big or small. I had become too ambitious for my own good, no doubt egged on by well-meaning ministers and authors who bang on about the need – indeed the moral imperative – to 'attempt great things for God'. Glory! I didn't fail as a missionary for the third time because I didn't try. There was no need. God was pleased with me whether I was a missionary or not. This discovery was the rekindling of hope for me.

No fear

But what if you are a Christian who really was called to serve God and somehow you have failed, and you are feeling apprehensive as a result? Well, there is hope for you. Other saints have been there, too. Paul points out: 'We are afflicted in every way, but not crushed; perplexed, but not driven to despair; persecuted, but not forsaken; struck down, but not destroyed; always carrying in the body the death of Jesus, so that the life of Jesus may also be manifested in our bodies' (Corinthians 4:8-10). Here are three promises found in Psalm 34:18-20, which I find helpful when I fail.

1. *The Lord is near to the broken-hearted, and saves the crushed in spirit* (18.) You are not alone in your pain,

despite how you feel. God is with you. I recommend meditating on this passage until you can see God with you.

2. *Many are the afflictions of the righteous; but the Lord delivers him out of them all.* (19) Far from being a people free from adversity, Christians can expect many afflictions, annoyances, calamities, misfortunes and failures.

3. *He keeps all his bones; not one of them is broken.* Notice this bit about no bones being broken (20). This refers to two things. First, God sets limits on our afflictions (See Job 2:6; 1 Corinthians 10:13). Also, it refers to the crucifixion of the Messiah whereby Jesus was subjected to failure as well. In his day, death on a cross was the ultimate failure. But death – and ultimately all failure – was eliminated by the resurrection.

OK. Looking optimistically ahead to the resurrection hardly removes the trauma we feel when we fail *now*. However, perhaps the situation will be eased if we shut our ears to Satan who accuses God of being uncaring and a liar. No matter how bleak our situation, we must remember that God is using our painful circumstances to bless us in the long run.

The swindle?

Are we to conclude, then, that the Bible's promises of success are a swindle, since Christians actually must endure failure and suffering like anyone else? Hardly. But there is one who would like us to believe it is. He would like us to curse God when we fail. This is the message of Job 2:4: 'Then Satan answered the Lord, "Skin for skin! All that a man has he will give for his life. But put forth thy hand now, and touch his bone and his flesh [or his bank account!], and he will curse thee to thy face.'" Job, of course, proved Satan wrong. It is the devil who is the true swindler! Satan wants us to believe that God doesn't care about our pain when we fail while serving him. And like most con jobs, Satan's lie is simple . . . and deadly. Don't let him swindle you.

1. Quoted with permission, 16 September 2001.
2. Lewis' poem 'Pilgrim's Problem' shows how he struggles with his sense of failure. Here he compares his life to a walker's map. He asks, 'Was the map wrong?' Lewis the pilgrim concludes he is not lost – that God's plans for his life, while not the plans he had made for himself, are infinitely better.
3. *The Practice of the Presence of God*, Brother Lawrence, Trans. E. M. Blaiklock, Hodder & Stoughton, 1981, p. 27.

CHAPTER TWO

Beware of unconfessed sin

By 1982, I had jam on it. I had married. I was teaching in a wonderful school in the United States. I enjoyed all the benefits a person could ask for: paid sick leave, lots of holidays, a good pension scheme, and a pleasant community in which to work. To most people, I probably appeared to be a very successful young man. And I was. I loved my wife. I enjoyed teaching. I belonged to a good church. But deep down I was frustrated. I felt God was calling me to be a writer.

During one of our many walks beneath the canopy of oak and pine trees that line the north-east shore of the Chesapeake Bay, my wife and I discussed the pros and cons of my returning to university to earn a master's degree in journalism. 'If you're sure that this is God's will,' Judith said cautiously, 'then I support the idea 100 per cent.'

Recalling the pain of my failed missionary calling, I retorted, 'Who can ever be certain of *that*?' As I watched the foam-flecked tide lap against the toes of my boots I picked up a stick and flung it out into the water. Then I bit my lower lip and admitted, 'I want to take this step of faith; only I'm too scared to actually do it.'

Judith was quiet.

Turning to face her, I pointed out, 'You know, if we decide to make the change, we'll have to give up all that we have now – our jobs, our friends, our security, everything – and begin all over again, knowing in the end there is no guarantee that I'll ever make a living as a writer. Are you willing to do that?'

'I'll tell you what,' said Judith in her pragmatic English way. 'You just apply to graduate schools now, and when the time comes, I'll go along with whatever you decide.' Later that year a letter dropped through our post box. Opening it hastily, I did a double take and let out a whoop. I had a place at university! My joy changed to apprehension. I tossed the letter aside. Now the question of living by faith was no longer hypothetical. Like Mother Teresa in 1946, and C. S. Lewis in 1954, we were about to exchange the predictable for the unknown.

The next day I drove down to the bay. There, I trudged along the beach until I came to an uprooted oak tree. Sitting on the trunk, I buried my bare feet in the cool sand and began to pray. As I did so, I spotted a sailboat on the horizon. The two-man crew tackled the strong breeze; sometimes they made good headway; other times they threatened to tip or come to a halt as they pressed towards the unseen shore across the water. Suddenly it seemed to me that God had revealed this picture to me so I would trust him. Like the small sailboat, we would be setting out to obey God's will. Right then and there, I decided to resign from my job and accept the place on my course. Looking back now, I think it is fair to say that if at the time I knew of the many failures that lay ahead, I might have lost the faith to do it.

To raise money for this new adventure, we sold our household items, keeping only bare essentials. After much thought, we decided to use part of our savings to pay for my first year of study rather than apply for a student loan.

For one thing, I was still paying off loans from my first degree, and we didn't want to add to this debt.

As a father would to his son

After an intense search in an unfamiliar but quaint mid-western town, we found quarters with a rent we could just afford – a basement maisonette. Our furniture consisted of a bed, a sofa, a shelf, a desk and two chairs, and some kitchen items. It was spartan but it was home. Judith worked as a receptionist at a publishing company, and I held down a variety of humdrum part-time jobs at the university.

We soon developed a pattern. Because my hours were erratic, I often sat up late studying with a pillowcase over a lamp while Judith slept. Our routine was destroyed, how-ever, when fumes from the ancient oil-fired central heating system made us sick and forced us out onto the street the night before the Thanksgiving holiday in the late autumn. Were it not for the kindness of friends who put us up, we might have spent a long and blustery November weekend sitting in our car.

After we complained about the fumes, our landlord claimed there was nothing wrong with the heating system, so we had to live with the fumes or leave. We heard of a spare bedroom that was for rent across town. Although the landlady was looking for a single working woman to rent, reluctantly she agreed that the two of us could move in with our few possessions.

That first year, we barely scraped by. The problem was money. The college announced an increase in fees for the next term. Over the summer, the college offered a special grant to mature students whose savings and incomes were below a certain level. We qualified for the grant in every respect but one: we had some money in the bank that had been given to us as a wedding gift. We had agreed to use the money only in an emergency (such as if Judi suddenly had to fly back to England). However, the amount we had made us ineligible for the grant by about two hundred dollars. Without telling my wife, I applied for the grant anyway, keeping quiet about the two hundred-dollar difference. 'God wants me to finish my degree,' I rationalised as I signed the forms. 'Otherwise he'd never have led us out here in the first place. And anyway, that's not money we earned. It's a gift.'

Although on paper we appeared to qualify for the grant, my application was rejected. After an initial period of disappointment, I found a better-paying part-time job in sales that allowed me to resume my studies. When the new term began, I buried myself in my work, forgetting about the lie I had told. But soon a series of bad events began to unfold. While playing baseball one evening, I broke a finger catching a sizzling line drive barehanded. Even with insurance we had to pay the doctor one hundred dollars for the treatment.

Next, my sales averages dropped off steadily, and as my salary was based on commissions, my paycheque began to shrink. I found I couldn't even give away the products. We moved rapidly from tightening our belts to almost being on the breadline! In the end, we had to use the remnant of our savings just to live. I began to wonder if I had heard God correctly when I gave up my secure teaching career.

The final blow came when our landlady gave us notice that we would have to move because her grandson needed a place to live. This was the second time we were homeless in a space of one year. We knew my dream of earning a master's degree was finished. In despair, I turned to God and cried, 'Why are you allowing this to happen to us, Lord?'

When we intentionally sin

When Christians knowingly sin, God needs to remind them of his total hatred of sin. In the Old Testament, Joshua fails, a man ordained by God to lead the chosen people into the Promised Land. Why? Because some men in his camp wilfully sin against God's holy law by taking some loot they shouldn't have taken. Joshua's brilliant military campaign ends in woeful defeat when the mighty Israelites are defeated while trying to capture the small city of Ai (Joshua 7:7, 10-12).

When Christians intentionally sin, God's action needs to be swift and conclusive, or else they will be doomed to more failure, even though they may be on a mission ordained by God himself. Simply stated, God is *holy*. The word holy appears 611 times in the Bible. Holiness is the predominant attribute of God and is basic to his nature and character. Since God is our father, he must punish inappropriate behaviour in his children.

Let's look at King David whom God referred to as a man after his own heart (1 Samuel 13:14). After many years of holy living, David became infatuated with Bathsheba, a married woman. David arranges to sleep with her even though he knows it is wrong. That night, she becomes pregnant. To try to cover up his sin, David orders the death of her husband, Uriah, one of David's most loyal military officers. By doing this, David adds betrayal and murder to adultery. Thinking he has now covered his wrongdoing, David takes Bathsheba as his wife and hopes the whole sordid affair will never come to light. But the prophet Nathan does not let him off lightly. Prompted by God, Nathan confronts David and tells him that retribution upon David and his household would follow; worse, all of Israel will know what David did (2 Samuel 12:9-12).

Don't cheapen grace

The New Testament is all about God's grace. Isn't retribution for sin strictly an Old Testament concept? No. In the New Testament, Ananias sells property and claims along with his wife Sapphira that he has given the money to the church. But he actually holds back a percentage of the proceeds for himself. Peter, receiving a word of knowledge from the Holy Spirit,[1] rebukes Ananias for lying (Acts 5:3). Peter points out that nobody forced Ananias to sell his property. It was something he decided to do of his own free will. Peter adds that it was not to men but to God he had lied (4). At these words, Ananias drops dead. Later, when Sapphira is given a chance to tell the truth, she lies, too, and she expires on the spot as well (7). Our holy God is the same yesterday, today and for ever (Hebrews 13:8).

Joshua, David, Ananias and Sapphira – their examples prove that God will send failure into people's lives to chastise them for unconfessed volitional sins. What's more, their stories speak volumes about the nature of the Christian's relationship with a holy God: God will not permit premeditated sinning among people who have told God he may take control of their lives.

When we know what is right, but we decide to do the wrong thing, God will cause us to fail in order to get us back on the right track. In my own case, my failures forced me to cast myself on my face before God (a position now very familiar to me!) I begged God to tell me why we had fallen on such hard times. Then God spoke to me. To be honest, I can't say I heard God's reply with my ears, but he clearly said, 'I allowed you to fail financially because you lied about your savings.'

Foolishly, I began to argue with God, pointing out that it was only a small sum of money, and anyway, the university didn't even give me the grant! Again, the voice said, 'I love you my son. I was very disappointed by your lack of faith in me.' This wasn't the thundering voice of an enraged Jehovah who stood poised with his fist clenched, ready to annihilate me. This was the still, gentle voice of my father in heaven, the one whom I had invited into my heart. The words of Hebrews came home clearly to me:

> And have you forgotten the exhortation which addresses you as sons? – 'My son, do not regard lightly the discipline of the Lord, nor lose courage when you are punished by him. For the Lord disciplines him whom he loves, and chastises every son whom he receives. It is for discipline that you have to endure. God is treating you as sons; for what son is there whom his father does not discipline?' (Hebrews 12:5-7)

I felt convicted and ashamed. Financial failure reminded me of God's intolerance of sin. I got off my face and went directly to my wife who had suffered along with me. I told her what I had done and what I felt God had said. We embraced, and then we fell down on our knees and I confessed to God. I didn't hear any reply this time, but I knew the matter had been settled and that the time of punishment was over. 'For God can use sorrow in our lives to help us turn away from sin and seek salvation. We will never regret that kind of sorrow. But sorrow without repentance is the kind that results in death' (2 Corinthians 7:10, NLT).

The Old Testament sums it up like this: 'If my people who are called by my name humble themselves, and pray and seek my face, and turn from their wicked ways, then I will hear from heaven, and will forgive their sin and heal their land' (2 Chronicles 7:14).

Since we both were on our knees, my wife asked God to provide a place for us to live. 'Lord, give us a place of beauty and stability,' she said. Although it was a modest request, I honestly didn't expect God to act so quickly. Within a fortnight, we were living in a rambling Victorian house not far from my university. We occupied two upstairs rooms with a private bathroom (talk about luxury!) Bas and Lynn and Matthew and Alisa, our landlords and their children, treated us like family for the rest of our time there.

Remember that God often sends failure into our lives in order to discipline Christians who knowingly abuse their Christian liberty. No one can predict what God will or will not do in different cases. Many times when we sin we are not punished because of grace. In any case, we must take care not to cheapen grace.

---

1. For more about 'words of knowledge', see Proverbs 23:12 and 1 Corinthians 12:8, the latter showing that Paul considered this one of the gifts of the Spirit.

CHAPTER THREE

The cracked mirror

Let's be clear about something terribly important. God tasted failure when he was nailed to the cross in the person of Jesus Christ. This is key, because through Jesus, God identifies with everyone who ever failed or will fail in this life. Pain and suffering are the legacy of Adam's fall. To borrow a phrase from Francis Schaeffer, sin 'cracked the image of God in man'. Schaeffer meant that while we are created in God's image, our nature is altered, like the distorted image in a cracked mirror, because of our sin. For those of us who are impatient with the by-product of sin – war, crime, disease, and failure – we may be certain that Christ, too, longed to end all suffering with a snap of his fingers. But because of our fallen nature, it has to be done the Father's way. That's why Jesus warned us that we would have to bear a cross from time to time: 'He who does not bear his cross and follow me is not worthy of me' (Matthew 10:38).

God wants Christians to carry our crosses so that, like Mother Teresa, we may identify with our shattered and hurting world. That's why we should not run from failure. Imagine India minus Mother Teresa. For millions of Indians, this would be unthinkable. Indians of all faiths and none turned out to mourn the passing of this tiny saint in 1997, a fact made all the more remarkable by the sectarian strife that normally divides the great religions of that nation. Yet her ministry very nearly came to an end in 1949.

Her diaries reveal that after a relatively short period of time working among the poorest of the poor in Calcutta's slums, she became discouraged by the slow progress and unspeakable working conditions. Feeling abandoned by God, this young woman longed to return to the sanity (and the sanitation!) of Europe, putting down her notion of serving Christ in India as a youthful fancy. She admits that everything she longed for was in Europe – pleasant society, beauty, comfort and prosperity. But history shows that she resisted this temptation to bolt, much the way Jesus resisted similar temptations in the desert (Luke 4:1-13), and again, the temptation to run from the crucifixion (Luke 22:42-44).

The heresy of the prosperity gospel

Ironically, for many of us today, the thought of carrying a cross in the service of our Lord is unthinkable. In fact, as the result of the liberties we enjoy through grace, there is a growing belief that God intends only the very best for his children – the best educations, the best homes, the best cars, the best jobs. The list could be endless. For a person to achieve anything less than the very best can mean only one thing in some Christian circles: loss of favour with the Father. Nothing can be further from the truth, which is why I call the Prosperity gospel heresy.

Many of us have been taken in to a certain extent by the lure of prosperity. We believe that a thriving congregation, a happy marriage, good health – success at whatever we undertake – is our right. And we become bitter towards God when we fail.

Many of us today live as if we are exempt from failures

by virtue of our faith. We pluck passages from the Bible (for example, Psalm 1), and then set out expecting to flourish, as if by magic. We have been taught to choose passages to back up our wishful thinking as well – for example Proverbs 3:6, *The Living Bible* puts it this way: 'In everything you do, put God first, and he will direct you, and crown your efforts with success.'

Of course, this is true in the strictest sense. After all, we should be able to point to times in our lives when God has blessed us with successes. But we are kidding ourselves if we select only the scriptures that promise health, wealth, and fulfilment, but ignore passages like Romans 2:9, which talk about accountability. Or Matthew 24:9-14 and John 15:18, which warn that there will be hardship and persecution for all who name Jesus as Lord and saviour. As for the idea that wealth is proof of God's blessing, how can we overlook Jesus' words in Matthew 8:20: 'And Jesus said to him, "Foxes have holes, and birds of the air have nests; but the Son of man has nowhere to lay his head."' Or Luke 6:20-21 which states: 'Blessed are the poor, for yours is the kingdom of God. Blessed are you who hunger now, for you shall be satisfied.'

Many Christian ministers demand outward proof from God that he is on their side. They teach that Christians should be the wealthiest people on our planet. Others teach that wealth and successes are the measure of our spiritual life. Those who support such beliefs are often highly vocal, commanding media attention, with large, dedicated followings. In reality, they are like the 'evil generation' Jesus rebuked in Luke 11:29: 'When the crowds were increasing, he began to say, "This generation is an evil generation; it seeks a sign, but no sign shall be given to it except the sign of Jonah."'

Using logic based on human reason, not the teaching of Christ, these leaders think they are improving God's reputation by insisting that God promises to deliver the faithful from the pains of social injustice, want, despair and failure. Such teachers ignore the fact that the founder of the faith, and all of the founding members, may be rightly called 'failures'. A *curriculum vitae* drawn up at the end of their lives would read like this:

- Criminal and found guilty of preaching sedition and sentenced to capital punishment; net worth, nil (Jesus).

- Failed fisherman, convicted criminal, put to death; net worth, nil (Peter).

- Failed tent maker, repeated instigator of riots, ex-convict, also put to death; net worth, nil (Paul).

- Vagabond given to seeing visions and exiled on Patmos. Net worth, nil (the apostle John).

- Mentally unstable prostitute turned Jesus groupie. Net worth, nil (Mary Magdalene).

The list goes on and on like this. You might say that deciding to follow God is one of the most foolish things you can do if worldly success is important to you.

In this day and age of Christian ministers who are more like spin-doctors, God has been remade in our image. But God cares nothing of our opinion of his sovereignty. In C. S. Lewis' *The Last Battle*, Aslan (a Christ symbol) appears to be uncaring about the hopeless plight of his Narnian followers. When the ancient holy trees are being cut down, apparently as the result of Aslan's orders, and the enemies of the Narnians – the Calormenes – are made masters of the land, serious questions regarding Aslan's goodness are raised. Even the faithful ones are ready to assume the worst about the mighty lion. Jewel, the unicorn, asks Tirian, the king of Narnia, how Aslan could be commanding such dreadful things? 'How should I know?' Tirian replies dryly. 'Aslan isn't a tame lion.'

Perhaps Lewis had in mind the lesson of suffering Job who, although innocent of any hidden sins, questioned God's goodness only to be humbled by God's imponderable reply: 'Shall a faultfinder contend with the Almighty?' (Job 40:2). Job was humbled by the reality of God's greatness and sovereignty in a way that few of us are today.

The Christian God is not a tame God. He does not necessarily act according to our human expectations of him, even though it seems right that he should. Joshua said to God after the unexpected defeat at Ai, 'For when the Canaanites and all the other people living in the land hear about it, they will surround us and wipe us off the face of the earth. And then what will happen to the honour of your great name?' (Joshua 7:9, NLT). This is the essence of the Prosperity gospel – excessive concern with outward appearances. God is in complete control of history, and his plan is for our good not our harm; meantime, he doesn't worry about public opinion polls.

The testimony of the scriptures and of countless men and women over the last two millennia proves God is with us in our pain. What appears to be a failure in the world's eyes may yet be used for our good if we trust God. That is the reality of John 3:16. God loves us. He is with us in our pain. Do not despair. As the fourteenth-century Christian mystic Mother Julian of Norwich succinctly put it: 'All will be well.' Smith Wigglesworth, the Pentecostal evangelist, echoes Julian's simplicity: 'Only believe and God will do the rest.'

Although it may be hard to comprehend, the successful Christian life must include a fair amount of failure. How can a Christian be a failure and a success at the same time? The successful Christian life is not one free from failure and pain, but one that can rejoice in and be transformed by failure. The Christian life is radically different. Consider the words of the apostle Paul: 'I know how to be abased, and I know how to abound; in any and all circumstances I have learned the secret of facing plenty and hunger, abundance and want. I can do all things in him who strengthens me' (Philippians 4:12-13). This is what I call the Christian success factor.

Failures are in good company

The apostle Paul was often criticised in his lifetime, being unfavourably compared to fellow Christian preachers who were more popular. One critic mocked him claiming that he was a greatly overrated lightweight. The apostle's reply? 'Oh, don't worry, I wouldn't dare say that I am as wonderful as these other men who tell you how good they are! Their trouble is they are only comparing themselves with each other . . . Our goal is to measure up to God's plan for us . . .' (2 Corinthians 10:12-13, *Living Bible*). This attitude epitomised Cliff Richard's position a few years ago when radio DJs announced that the star who practically defined the pop genre in the UK was no longer fit for their play lists. Instead of sulking or running to his lawyers, Cliff countered by performing the 'Lord's Prayer' in time for the Millennium celebrations. To the best of my knowledge, that song didn't make the radio play lists, but it still became a bestseller in the shops.

Sir Cliff and St Paul know that worldly acclaim means

nothing to God. He made us and loves us whether the world says we are failures or not. He hears us and comforts us when we turn to him in pain. One sure way for me to feel a like a failure is to compare my meagre book sales to those of Adrian Plass. But when I do this, the Holy Spirit gently explains to me that I should concentrate on how I appear to God not the Christian booksellers. Call me naïve, but this brings me great comfort.

God knows we are prone to failure. Look at the great men and women of faith in the Bible. How many escaped the bracing slaps of defeat as they tried to live their lives for God and his kingdom? When Moses and the Jews marched triumphantly out of bondage in Egypt, leaving an awe-struck Pharaoh in their wake, or when the zealous apostle Peter amazed his friends by venturing out on the Sea of Galilee on foot, both these men were pressing towards failure. God preserved a written record of these tragedies to remind us that because of our fallen nature very few saints get through this life unscathed. I don't know about you, but I am glad that my failures aren't immortalised in a best seller like the Bible for all generations to see!

The locust years

Knowing that biblical men and women have also failed may do little to restore your equilibrium when your plans turn sour. To fail is a serious blow to a Christian's faith. When it happens, we feel cheated, hurt, and angry. However, we must resist self-pity, a dangerous emotion. Satan, who understands failure only too well as the result of his own fall from grace (see Revelation 12:7-9), is always ready to grind us down. A limited creature unable to see the future, Satan uses our current pain to try to push us to the brink of despair and beyond. But God, who sees the future, delights in drawing straight lines with crooked sticks, and so he promises all who have felt defeated:

> The threshing floors shall be full of grain, the vats shall overflow with wine and oil. I will restore to you the years which the swarming locust has eaten, the hopper, the destroyer, and the cutter, my great army, which I sent among you. You shall eat in plenty and be satisfied, and praise the name of the Lord your God, who has dealt wondrously with you. And my people shall never again be put to shame (Joel 2:24-26).

CHAPTER FOUR

Shattered dreams

There was no doubt about it. It was foot and mouth disease. John Evans (not his real name), an organic farmer in Llangenny, found one of his cows salivating heavily. When he saw this, he knew the dreaded epidemic had caught up with him despite his careful farming methods. Within one week, nine more cases were reported in Llangenny, an area previously thought free of the disease. Farmers there had believed Government reports that the plague was over. Now they all watched and prayed as their livelihoods ended in mass culling of cattle, sheep, and goats.

Foot and mouth may be a thing of the past now, but during the summer of 2001, 3,577,000 animals were slaughtered, with thousands more awaiting destruction. There were a total of 8,811 known affected premises in the UK, with new ones appearing monthly.

Farmers like John Evans put their best efforts into running humane and clean animal farms. But through no fault of their own, their livelihoods were ruined by something as capricious as airborne spores from another farm. Christian farmers have suffered along with their non-believing neighbours as the result of the foot and mouth disease. So how come God allows this to happen?

From time to time, failure is the result of facing insurmountable difficulties, given our natural limitations. When this happens to us, how may we find a way forward? In a word, *trust*.

Lemonade anyone?

An American humorist once said that if life gives you a lemon, make lemonade.

Eric Liddell, Scotland's star runner of the 1924 Paris Olympic Games, was handed a particularly bitter lemon when he was ordered to run on the Sabbath – something his staunch Calvinistic upbringing would not allow him to do. He had to decide between honouring his country or compromising his faith.

Liddell had first captured the attention of the sporting world by giving up his successful rugby career to train as an Olympic runner. Against all odds, he established himself as a first-rate sprinter with an unusual head-back running style that he called running for the 'glory of God'. Eric was written up in all the papers as Britain's best hope for a gold medal.

Only after this highly competitive young Scot had travelled to Paris did he learn that he had been scheduled to run his event on a Sunday. After many agonising hours of prayer and introspection, he decided not to run. Consequently, the unsympathetic press had a heyday with him, and his own team considered him to be a traitor. It would have been understandable if he had recanted and gone ahead with the Sunday event in the light of the bashing that he took for his religious beliefs.

Someone once said that when God closes a door, he opens a window. In the end, a window of opportunity was thrown open to Liddell. A team-mate offered to step aside to allow Liddell to run a different race in his place on a weekday, and the Flying Scotsman, as he had been dubbed by the international press, accepted. Eric Liddell won the race, securing a Gold for Britain, and returned to Britain in triumph. Because this athlete was determined to honour God, God honoured him.

Significantly, Liddell didn't allow the acclaim of the sporting world to turn his head. Following his brief Olympic career, Liddell joined his family as a missionary in China during the dark days leading up to the Second World War. Not long after the Japanese invaded China, Liddell was taken prisoner and confined to a spartan POW compound for the duration of the war. Yet even in these harsh circumstances, Eric Liddell found that all things do work for good for those who love God and are called to his purposes. Many people alive today have written about Liddell's joyful giving of himself in the prison camp. He organised sports, social activities, and Bible studies for the many bored teens and children who were also held captive during the war years. Sadly, there was no happy ending to this tale. Eric Liddell became ill and died a depressing death in an obscure POW camp in China.

Pride precedes a fall

Sometimes circumstances beyond our control, combined with our own personal shortcomings, lead to failure. The failed politician Jonathan Aitken lived through the hell of seeing the details of his private life spread across the headlines of the nation's press in the run-up to his futile libel action and his subsequent trial for perjury and attempting to pervert the course of justice. But he has begun to turn his life around since his remarkable fall from grace in the late 1990s.

In his autobiography *Pride and Perjury* (HarperCollins, 2000), Aitken admits that his arrogance had led to his undoing. He writes about how his worst failures have since become his greatest teacher. Today he says he is grateful for his failure.[1] The man who was once tipped to become the next leader of the Conservative Party now sits at Jesus' feet, desiring to grow as a human being.

Without excusing his malfeasances, I am struck by the man he has become as the result of his personal and political failings. Clearly, his political career is dead, but his new life – a life of service to others – is just beginning.

Where do people like Eric Liddell and Jonathan Aitken find the inner strength to live victorious lives despite their crushing failures?

Simple. The Holy Spirit.

Our personal counsellor

'If you love me, you will keep my commandments. And I will pray to the Father, and he will give you another Counsellor, to be with you for ever' (John 14:15-16). Most people know me to be an easy-going sort of man that likes to laugh a lot. But some who knew me years ago will recall me as a time bomb waiting to go off. My problem was that I didn't believe God loved me. My many failures proved it to me – or so I thought.

You often hear the term 'the fatherhood of God'. Ironically, although I was born again and therefore an adopted son of God, for years I felt more like one of the 'neighbourhood kids' in God's community. You know what I mean. When neighbourhood kids are visiting with your children, you look after them, but at a certain point, you ask them to leave, so you may feed your kids, read them stories, do homework with them, hug them, and then tuck them up in their own comfortable beds. In my mind, I was just a stray kid in God's neighbourhood. But no longer. Today, I feel like a son and heir. So what transformed me?

It all began in mid-1989. After church one Sunday, my friend Hilary stopped me. She looked into my eyes and asked, 'How are you?' I prepared to give her a stock answer, when I surprised myself by admitting that I was feeling very scared.

'Of what?' she asked.

'Of failure,' I said. 'Bills, family life, my work, my health. No matter how much I pray, nothing's right. It's as if God hates me.' I wondered if my words surprised her, as at the time, I was a successful Christian author, a BBC religious correspondent, and a lay preacher. But Hilary didn't bat an eyelid.

'Oh, you need to know more about Jesus,' she said earnestly. 'Ask him what's missing in your life and he'll show you.' Annoyed by her pat advice, I thanked her and stamped away.

While visiting family in Devon that Christmas, I faced a deep personal crisis. With tears streaming down my cheeks, I walked to the seafront where a December storm was pummelling the shore. I climbed onto a breakwater and thought about ending it all. Then I recalled Hilary's advice: 'You need to know more about Jesus.' I cried out into the icy wind, 'OK, God. If I need to know more about Jesus, show me what you want me to know!' These were the words God had been waiting for me to proclaim for years.

Next day, I went to church and heard a sermon about coping with failure. Thinking the vicar might help me get to know Jesus better, I arranged to meet him at his home.

He was very kind. Over tea, I unburdened my problems. After hearing me out, he frankly admitted that he, too, was deluged with problems – many seemingly insurmountable. He sighed, concluding, 'Maybe God is disciplining us in order to build our character.' This wasn't what I was expecting.

Feeling despondent after this meeting, I went for a walk. 'Is he right, Lord?' I thought. 'I'm a father. I understand the need to discipline my children. But sometimes they just need loving. If you love me, please help me.'

In my work as a broadcaster, I had recently interviewed Albert Taylor, a Christian counsellor. He talked about deliverance ministry and healing of the emotions, things that I had never heard of before. After the interview, I remarked to my wife that if anyone could help me, it would be this man. So in January, behind my back, my wife rang him and an appointment was made which I only reluctantly agreed to keep.

Albert and his wife Elisabeth listened to my problems and prayed with me. Afterwards he said, 'I think I can help.' My ears pricked up. 'You need a special kind of ministry called healing of the memories.'

At first I rejected his opinion, saying that there is no mention of this term in the Bible. Moreover, I said, Christians are new creatures immune to past hurts and demonic influences. But even great saints have fallen prey to forces like the ones St Paul described in Ephesians 6:12 – 'principalities and powers . . . wicked hosts in the heavenly places.'[2]

If I'm honest, many of my problems stemmed from past events – the death of my father, rejections, various failures – all of which left deep emotional scars on me. Moreover, I had told God he could teach me more about himself. Perhaps this was what he wanted me to know. So, reluctantly, I acquiesced.

To make a long story short, through Albert's ministry, Jesus freed me from sad memories that had dominated my life. After a few sessions, I no longer woke up feeling depressed, but more importantly, I became acutely aware of God's love for me. This transformed my whole life.

Over the next few weeks, Albert broached the baptism in the Holy Spirit. As I had been taught against accepting this as a legitimate doctrine, I was wary. 'I already have the Holy Spirit,' I argued. 'He comes in full measure at the moment you become a Christian.' However, as inner healing had helped me – my wife said I was like a new man – perhaps this was something else I needed. So I knelt and asked for the baptism of the Holy Spirit. Nothing happened.

A few weeks later, on the afternoon of 14 February, Valentine's Day 1990, I decided to ask again for the baptism in the Holy Spirit. Hands were laid on me, and my friends began to pray. At first, nothing happened. Gradually, a dark mist seemed to envelop me. Minutes later, as they continued to pray, brilliant silver light pierced the darkness, causing the blackness to evaporate. I knew that the Holy Spirit had entered my life in a new way.

What a difference this experience has made in me. First of all, I began to pray in tongues. Glory! They hadn't ceased as I had been taught. My fear of tongues was that I could be defaming Jesus in a demonic utterance. Far from uttering demonic curses, my experience tells me that when I pray in tongues, I'm expressing faith in Jesus Christ as God (1 Corinthians 12:3).

Better than tongues, though, is my new boldness to put on the full armour of which St Paul spoke. Week by week, anxieties and doubts fell away like broken shackles. For years, I had been cynical and emotionally drained. But now, I am no longer a neighbourhood kid. I'm a part of the family of God, a child assured of Father God's love.

If as the result of endless failures, you feel you could do with knowing more about Jesus, don't be timid. Boldly ask him what he wants to reveal to you. Knock and it shall be opened; ask and you shall receive. Of course, I'm not saying that following my experiences failure simply dried up and blew away. I finally understood how to engage the enemy. Let's unpack St Paul's teaching on the full armour of God.

> Put on all of God's armour so that you will be able to stand firm against all strategies and tricks of the Devil. For we are not fighting against people made of flesh and blood, but against the evil rulers and authorities of the unseen world, against those mighty powers of darkness who rule this world, and against wicked spirits in the heavenly realms. Use every piece of God's armour to resist the enemy in the time of evil, so that after the battle you will still be standing firm. Stand your ground, putting on the sturdy belt of truth and the body armour of God's righteousness. For shoes, put on the peace that comes from the Good News, so that you will be fully prepared. In every battle you will need faith as your shield to stop the fiery arrows aimed at you by Satan (Ephesians 6:11-16, NLT).

Isn't the apostle warning us that the Christian life is the life of a warrior? If so, we can expect the ceaseless attacks of the devil, which display themselves through our own sin, failures, and the temptations set before us by the world. If it weren't so, Paul would have told us to put on the dressing gown of complacency, the bedroom slippers of the gospel, and snooze soundly in the easy chair of life until the Second Coming.

Faith of a mustard seed

Jesus said faith the size of a mustard seed is sufficient for this life. Perhaps you think even this is more than you can assemble. Maybe. Yet, don't we demonstrate greater faith every day? It takes faith (some would say stupidity!) to send credit card details via the Internet, or to post an important document to a distant place. It takes great faith to try a new medicine, or to board a plane or a train for a long journey. I don't conduct a full investigation into a coach driver's driving record before I agree to let him speed me along the motorway in bumper-to-bumper traffic. I just exercise faith that all will be well.

If we are able to have so much faith in man-made systems that we *know* are bound to fail, shouldn't we be willing to have faith in a God who will never fail us? 'Have no anxiety about anything, but in everything by prayer and supplication with thanksgiving let your requests be made known to God. And the peace of God, which passes all understanding, will keep your hearts and your minds in Christ Jesus' (Philippians 4:6-7).

Responding to the charge of a well-known atheist that Christianity has failed to live up to its claims to transform society, G. K. Chesterton replied, 'The problem is not that Christianity has been tried and found wanting; it's that Christianity has never been tried.' Sadly, Chesterton might well be talking to the Church of the twenty-first century.

The myth of the messiah complex

Psychiatrists have coined the term 'messiah complex' to describe the condition of certain people who actually desire to fail. The idea is that Jesus somehow wanted to go to the cross. But this is a monstrous distortion of the character of Christ. Christ's agony in the garden is proof that he didn't want to die. In fact, he fell on his face and prayed to God, saying, 'My Father, if it is possible, let this cup pass from me' – because nobody in his right mind desires to suffer.

However, the object lesson for the believer comes to us in Jesus' next breath – 'nevertheless, not as I will, but as thou wilt' (Matthew 26:39).

Sadly, many do not grasp the significance of Christ's sacrificial love. Christ's life would indeed be the tragedy ascribed to it by many had it not been for the miracle of the empty tomb. Historically, the victory on the cross has meant only one thing for people – joy! As the apostle Paul put it: 'Death is swallowed up in victory. O death, where is thy victory? O death, where is thy sting?' (1 Corinthians 15:55).

We may be confident that in all things God is working for the good of his children. In the meantime, God speaks to us through our circumstances, whether we succeed or fail. Our motto must be: 'Not my will but yours, God.' This isn't a messiah complex; it's a faithful response to a loving God who 'turns the rock into a pool of water, the flint into a spring of water.' (Psalm 114:8) To believe this, however, requires faith.

For many, faith is like a set of instructions I once saw on a box of holiday candles: 'Do not light. For decoration only.' If your faith is cold, if your life is dominated by fear more than joy, if you are content to sit in church Sunday by Sunday without seeing the power of Christ's love in action, then perhaps, like Chesterton's charge, you have not yet tried Christianity. Break open the candles of your faith and light them! Being a Christian is about having faith. Faith produces confidence, assurance and certainty – even when all seems to be lost. Don't let fear immobilise you. All that is required to operate in faith is that we make the first move. Then God does the rest.

When I was younger, I worked as a lifeguard with an

Outward-Bound type of camp. I recall coming to the aid of a distressed swimmer who, rigid with fear, was unable to pull himself out of the Susquehanna River, a swift and deep Pennsylvania waterway. All he could do was hang onto a rock near the shore as the water cascaded over him. He was afraid to reach any higher than the first rock he could reach. I knew that if I didn't get him out of the water he could drown.

I jumped in behind him. Because the lad was twice my size, I couldn't push him out; I could only support him in the water. I knew if I could get him to make the first move, he would be saved. After talking to him for a while, he agreed to reach his hands up higher. As he did, I pushed him up. With the help of some people on the riverbank, he came out like a cork out of a bottle! Sometimes, this is how faith works. Scary as it may be, we have to co-operate with God, so he can do the rescuing. Here are six ways you may help God to help you:

1. Don't stop praying when you feel scared or depressed. More good is accomplished through prayer than we'll ever know in this life.

2. Begin a new quest to discover the parts of the Bible you don't yet know. To do this, you should spend time reading your Bible each day. I am always amazed to discover some kernel of wisdom that I hadn't seen before, often containing the very words I need at that time.

3. Act on your Bible knowledge. In other words, what you see the saints doing, you do.

4. Think of eternity, not just the here and now. We put far too much stock in this life. I have kept a journal more or less every day since August 1976. From time to time,

I look back at what I wrote as a young man. I see that over the decades, many problems have come and gone – many of them I can hardly recall now. Yet Satan makes us think that our current failures will blight us for ever. They won't. Whatever is troubling you today, *this too shall pass.*

5. Learn from your failures. King David's many lapses from grace allowed him to gain the wisdom to compose many of the Psalms. Wisdom is born of failure!

6. Be proactive. Turn your grief into joy by serving others worse off than yourself. No matter how badly off we are, there's always someone else in a worse situation who needs our help.

As you do this, God will be at work in your own life, helping you to cope with your own failures.

1. Jonathan Aitken, *Pride and Perjury*, HarperCollins, London, 2000, p. 358.
2. On Wednesday, 5 September 2001, CNN reported that Mother Teresa needed deliverance ministry during her later years. According to the report, Henry D'Souza, the Archbishop of Calcutta, observed the late nun in an 'extremely agitated' state while she was hospitalised for cardiac problems. She would appear perfectly placid during the day, then toss and turn at night, pulling off the monitoring wires that were attached to her arms. D'Souza diagnosed Mother Teresa as suffering from demonic oppression. The solution? – to have the rite of exorcism performed, the Catholic term for deliverance ministry. Under other circumstances, Mother Teresa might not have agreed to undergo deliverance ministry. But because of her failed health, she agreed. The Archbishop called in a minister, and in the power of the Holy Spirit, he commanded the evil spirits to leave the elderly woman alone. After the ministry, D'Souza says, Mother Teresa 'slept like a baby'.

CHAPTER FIVE

Deo proviso!

Uncle Joe Pecci told me this story only a few months before he died. He reached over to hold my Aunt Sofie's hand and said, 'You know, Sofie and I have been married for over fifty years. But we almost didn't tie the knot!' Sofie shook her head and shrugged her shoulders. 'The same day I asked her to marry me,' he said, 'my boss fired me.'

This was in Depression-era America, 1930. Work was scarce, and times were tough. There were ten more years before prosperity was to return, and millions of men were without jobs. 'So, I cleared my desk and walked slowly home past Sophie's gate,' Uncle Joe continued. 'She was standing there waiting for me as usual. "Sofie," I said, "I got fired today." She made round eyes. "Do you still want to marry me, my girl?" I asked. Sofie, all of 19, nodded her head and said, "Oh, yes, Joe. Let's. But how will we live?"' Uncle Joe's high-pitched laugh rolled across the table. 'You know what I said to Sofie?' he asked me. 'The same thing I've been saying for the last fifty years: *Deo proviso* – God provides!'

On a Tuesday a few weeks before Christmas 1995, I had just come off air at the London radio station where I worked. I knew my programme had gone well, so I was feeling a buzz that only live radio gives. A cryptic note on my desk asked that I call in to see the acting station manager. I had helped this man to get a job with our station, but he had been rapidly promoted ahead of me. I felt bad for him for he had been asked to do the impossible. After only nine months of broadcasting our radio station was in dire financial straits. His task was somehow to keep the station on air. It was an awfully big task

I knew that change was in the air, and I supposed that he wanted to consult me about what would be the best way forward for everyone concerned. I knocked on the door of his new office. 'Come in. Have a seat.' Awkward silence. 'This is turning out to be the worst day of my life,' he groaned. I remained silent. 'Mike, I have to let you go. We can't afford you any more.'

The words ricocheted in my head. I hadn't expected this. I had left the BBC to come to this job, making personal and financial sacrifices to do it. I had a family and a mortgage, and my wife was a stay-at-home mum. Suddenly I felt as if my life was on fire. I couldn't find any words, so I stood up, thanked him and walked out.

The bracing slap of being sacked stayed with me on the journey home. But as I rounded into our driveway, I thought of my Uncle Joe and Aunt Sofie. What was it he used to say when times got tough? *Deo proviso!*

I lost my job in December 1995 and haven't had a full-time job since then, just a series of contracts. Nevertheless, I have not had to go on the dole. I have not had to borrow money. And there has always been food, friends and laughter around our table. *Deo proviso!* But how?

Partly by human means. Many sympathetic editors have commissioned me to write articles and books, so much so, that I have reinvented myself as a print journalist rather than a broadcaster. Several people here and abroad gave us substantial gifts of money when they heard what had happened. A former employer has given me regular, albeit part-time work. My father-in-law Reg Simms and brother-in-law David Harrison and his wife Jane generously helped us with our mortgage twice. Our church has rallied around us wonderfully, getting the right balance between leaving us alone and being there when we needed them.

Taken in isolation, these acts of charity aren't enough to sustain a family facing a crisis. Collectively, however, they have had the same effect as the two fishes and five loaves of bread in Matthew 14:17.

God made other miracles happen, too. Mainly in my heart. Mercifully, I'm not angry at my former employers. Better still, I'm not feeling sorry for myself. Best of all, I have had the opportunity to teach my children what Uncle Joe taught me – *Deo proviso*, God provides. As a family, we sometimes talk about ourselves in the way we might talk about characters in a book that we've read, and have seen in the end that, despite many painful conflicts, everything works out for the best.

It's God's fault

Why would a loving God want anyone to suffer as the result of some painful episode? American New Age guru, Gore Vidal, once said that the God of the Bible was the ultimate source of evil. He added the sooner the Bible religion was banned, the sooner global peace would come about.

Vidal was merely echoing what the atheistic French philosopher Albert Camus wrote in *The Plague*. Protagonist Pere Paneloux pronounces that the bubonic plague originates as a punitive act of God. Thus, as Camus sees it, if we attempt to resist evil, we are forced to choose between fighting God (who created the plague) or joining God in persecuting humans by passively accepting evil.

What Camus may not have realised is that Jesus hates the plague, too. More importantly, to demonstrate his solidarity with us, he became a man and endured his own tragic death on a cross to demonstrate once and for all his ultimate love for human beings. In doing so, he threw open the formerly barred gateway to eternal life. This is what gives us our ultimate hope: 'For God so loved the world that he gave his only son that whoever believes in him should not perish but have eternal life' (John 3:16).

But if God is all-powerful, he could wave his hand, and in a moment, all human failure would end. True, however, the Bible is God's Word, not a collection of folktales designed to make us feel good.

God's Word is big on realism. Nowhere in it are we given a promise that we will not have problems in this life. In fact, the opposite seems true – at least for people who call themselves Christians. Nevertheless, St Paul gives us hope. He said that the problems believers endure – while painful – have only a limited capacity to harm us. Ultimately, God's love will rescue us and comfort us: 'Who shall separate us from the love of Christ? Shall tribulation, or distress, or persecution, or famine, or nakedness, or peril, or sword? Nor height, nor depth, nor anything else in all creation will be able to separate us from the love of God in Christ Jesus our Lord' (Romans 8:35, 39).

Failure is a form of godly discipline

I want to suggest that in addition to what we've considered in the previous four chapters, God uses failure to *protect* those whom he loves from sin. Sin has many definitions in the scriptures, including 'rebellion', 'missing the mark', 'having a broken relationship with God', 'ungodliness', 'perversion' and so on. Put simply, sin separates us from the one we need more than anyone else; sin separates us from God.

The book of Exodus presents clear evidence that God provides for his people.

It also teaches us that human beings are utterly sinful. Because of our depravity, God must teach us that we are to be totally dependent on him. Failure is one of his lesson plans.

After God rescued the Jews from plagues, pestilence, and death in Egypt (Exodus 6-16), Moses persuaded Pharaoh to allow the Jews to exit Egypt. To speed them on their way, God put a pillar of smoke and fire before them to guide the Jews to their destination. He supplied them with manna to eat until they reached the Promised Land. And if this was not enough, he parted the waters of the Red Sea so they could escape the army of an enraged Pharaoh (Exodus 13-14).[1] Through these signs and wonders, God made it clear that the Jews were meant to depend on him for their welfare. And as long as things were tough, the Jews complied.

Beginning in Exodus 16, however, life for the Jews became much easier. Soon, they forgot about the need to depend on God. This is what author Bob Gass refers to as 'financial amnesia'. We remember God in times of crisis but forget him as soon as they are over. We can't count our blessings because we are too busy counting our money (or some other outward form of prosperity). In good times, we may feel as if we don't need God as much, because everything is going our way.[2] That's when sin takes over our lives.

The Jews' sins reached critical mass when Moses came down from Mount Sinai and found his brother Aaron leading God's people in a debauched feast honouring a golden idol whom the Jews proclaimed had led them out of Egypt. So great was their sin that they ascribed their deliverance to a false god! 'And he received the gold at their hand, and fashioned it with a graving tool, and made a molten calf; and they said, "These are your gods, O Israel, who brought you up out of the land of Egypt!"'(Exodus 32:4). How did God react? God sent failure to dominate the lives of his chosen people for the next 40 years as a means of keeping them faithful. Sin and human nature haven't changed since Moses' day. Neither have God's methods.

Tough love

When a disease attacks our body, the central nervous system generates an electronic stimulus known as pain. The pain alerts us to treat a malady before it grows out of control and kills us. Uncomfortable as pain may be, it's a good thing we are designed this way, because we could die without an early warning system.

I don't know a lot about leprosy, but I do know it is a disease that not only disfigures the extremities of the body, but it deadens pain. Author Philip Yancy points out that some lepers don't lose their sense of pain, and for this they are grateful. This is because pain helps them avoid life-threatening diseases or injuries. Similarly, we ought to be grateful that God allows us to fail from time to time, because the pain of defeat may drive us from going further into our sin.

We ought not to think we Christians are uniquely spared from failure. We hear so much about 'tough love' these days, as if it is a new idea. God invented tough love, a love that dares to discipline if it will bring us back to him when we stray. The Old and New Testaments bear this out: 'So you should realise that just as a parent disciplines a child, the Lord your God disciplines you to help you' (Deuteronomy 8:5, NLT). 'For the Lord disciplines those he loves, and he punishes those he accepts as his children' (Hebrews 12:6, NLT). This is God's Word. And although God grieves with us in our pain, he will not override his own Word.

Out of failure comes success

My friend Terry has been married three times, has had a string of failed businesses, and lives with a permanent back problem. One day he said to me, 'Life is good.' He looked around at his modest home, his healthy family, and his many other blessings. Then he added, 'All this and heaven, too!' That's how we may feel, even when life gets us down. Failure is a part of life, but as Christians, our failures need not rob us of contentment. In fact, each time we fail, we have a unique opportunity to succeed in our highest calling in this life – teaching others about Jesus Christ (Matthew 28:18-20). Let me explain.

Stephen was a first-century disciple who looked after the needs of the widows. He was endowed with faith, he was full of grace, he exercised spiritual gifts, and he demonstrated great wisdom (Acts 6:5, 8, 10). Clearly, Stephen's job was very important.

Soon, however, the local synagogue became upset with Stephen, and the Sanhedrin charged him with blasphemy. At his trial, he claimed to see Jesus standing at the right hand of God. For this, he was seized and duly stoned to death. What a terrible waste! It was a tragedy for Stephen's family. It was a disaster for the early Church. And it meant that the widows would be worse off than ever before. Yet out of this miscarriage of justice we see something very good happening. Saul of Tarsus assisted in Stephen's execution, and it was then that Saul first saw the power of the Christian God. Stephen was tranquil as the rocks crushed the life out of him (Acts 7:58, 59). Not long after, Saul's eyes were opened, and he became Paul, a follower of Christ, an evangelist, a miracle worker, and, of course, a man who followed Stephen's example of going to his own death peacefully.

Dietrich Bonhoeffer, a Christian minister, was so appalled by the persecution of the Jews in Germany, that he joined a plot to assassinate Hitler. The plot failed, and Bonhoeffer was arrested and hung in April 1945. As it was so near the end of the war, and Hitler was soon to take his own life in his bunker at the junction of the Wilhelmstrasse and Unter den Linden in Berlin, you could say this Lutheran minister's life ended in a tragic failure. *On the contrary.* The Nazi doctor who was present at Bonhoeffer's execution later said he had never seen a man die so peacefully, so entirely submissive to God's will. In death, Bonhoeffer passed on life to a spiritually dead Nazi doctor, who in turn passed on his faith to countless others. Success emerges out of failure!

If you are currently facing some great trail, some heart-breaking failure, here are three reasons why you mustn't lose sleep over it.

- First, it will pass.

- Second, it has the potential to draw you closer to God.

- Third, with God's help, some good will come of it.

Remember, the way in which you conduct yourself in hard times has the potential to impress even the most ardent unbelievers. Since this is so, this may give us courage to face whatever the future holds. Meantime, *Deo proviso!*

1. I am aware that there are many Christians who consider the Exodus story to be myth. Yet modern archaeology is making open-minded sceptics think again about the historicity of the Bible. If you'd care to find out more about this, see Jeffery Sheler's book *Is the Bible True?* (HarperCollins, 1999).

2. Bob Gass, *The Word for Today*, November-December-January 2001, Thursday, 1 November, p. 3. *The Word for Today* is published by United Christian Broadcasters and available free of charge from PO Box 225, Stoke-on-Trent, ST4 8YY, UK.

CHAPTER SIX

A pyramid of paradoxes

It's a contradiction. A genuine *paradox*. Why do people think Christianity is joyless? Historically, the Christian faith has meant only one thing – joy! Joy is defined in the *Concise Oxford Dictionary* as: Vivid emotion of pleasure, gladness; a thing that causes delight. In no other world religion and in no other literature is joy so conspicuous as in Christianity and in the Bible.

Let's look at some examples. 'Happy are those who hear the joyful call to worship, for they will walk in the light of your presence, Lord' (Psalm 89:15, *The Living Bible*). Jesus states that keeping God's commandments is the basis of living in loving relationships. 'These things I have spoken to you, that my joy may be in you, and that your joy may be full' (John 15:10-11). The references to joy in the Bible go on and on. Take a Bible concordance and look up the word 'joy'. You will find dozens of verses to support the fact that God wants us to be a cheerful people.

Of eggs and carrots

1 Thessalonians 1:6 sheds light on how we may have joy even in the midst of hardship: '. . . for you received the word in much affliction, with joy inspired by the Holy Spirit.' Here Paul teaches that one of the many manifestations

of the Holy Spirit is *joy*. Joy is also the fruit of our faith referred to in Galatians 5:22: 'But the fruit of the Spirit is love, joy, peace, patience, kindness, goodness, faithfulness . . .' This means there is a supernatural joy agent at work on our behalf in the midst of our suffering. Since none of us are cheerful in a catastrophe, how may we have joy when we are in pain through some misadventure?

Few people will be able to forget the hellish scenes of the World Trade Centre atrocity. Thousands of people lost their lives and thousands more lost friends or loved ones. And yet, paradoxically, in the midst of so much suffering and pain, the Holy Spirit was at work even there.

Chaplains bravely rushed into the inferno alongside fire-fighters and police, with at least one, Fr Mychal Judge, a chaplain with the New York City Fire Department, laying down his life in order to administer last rites to the dying. News magazines carried stories of US citizens going beyond their individual selfish desires to help each other out, and start to get a sense of true priorities. The Rev Billy Graham boldly shared the good news of Jesus Christ with a global audience of a billion-plus men, women and children during a memorial service on 14 September. President George W. Bush designated that same day as a National Day of Prayer and Remembrance, while here in Europe a three-minute period of silence was observed and prayers were said for the families of the dead. In fact, more people have been going to church since 11 September.[1] As in previous wars, hard circumstances drive people to seek God for answers to life's disappointments.

Without wanting to be flippant, I recall something that evangelist J. John once said of human misery. He compared it to boiling water, adding, 'Boiling water hardens an egg but it softens a carrot.' Of course, these few examples do not suggest that the aftermath of 11 September was rapturous joy in the face of human misery. But no one can deny that such expressions of love and faith have the effect of softening not hardening us – even in the midst of such wanton destruction.

Like children

If we allow the troubles of this world to harden our attitudes, then we are missing out on an important peculiarity of our faith – the call to be childlike. What are children like? Go to any playground and you will see for yourself – they are joyful, trusting, happy and innocent. Children laugh hundreds of times a day; adults laugh a great deal less. This is because children don't dwell on past mistakes. They move on and live for the moment. Children are not self-conscious, so they find joy in the smallest things. Introspection keeps adults focused on the negative and robs us of joy.

Once Jesus was attending to the pressing needs of a crowd when some children were presented to him. Squirming like a batch of puppies, the children charged towards Jesus. As soon as the disciples saw this, they tried to shoo the children away. But to everyone's astonishment, Jesus wanted the children to remain:

> He said to them, 'Let the children come to me. Don't stop them! For the Kingdom of God belongs to such as these. I assure you, anyone who doesn't have their kind of faith will never get into the Kingdom of God' (Mark 10:14-15, NLT).

Here, then, is another paradox: The older we become, the more we need to be childlike.

C. S. Lewis, a man who knew grief well, frequently used the metaphor of Christ presiding over a holiday feast to convey the Christian life. If your image of Jesus is of a peevish, depressing little man, it's been influenced by generations of bad art and prudery. If Jesus were really a killjoy, children would have wailed as their embarrassed parents struggled to set them on his lap. The opposite is true. Kids queued up to chat with Jesus like modern-day children pressing in to visit Father Christmas in a department-store grotto. Why? It stands to reason that Christ was a witty and pleasant man to be around.

The humour of Christ

Here is still another paradox: Christ is described as well acquainted with grief and failure (Isaiah 53:3), yet he was still able to generate *la joie de vivre* that drew all sorts of people to him – rich and poor, educated and uneducated, big and small. How did he do it?

In Mark 10:25, when Jesus said: 'It is easier for a camel to go through the eye of a needle than for a rich man to enter the kingdom of God', he was making an absurd pun along the lines of 'What weighs two tonnes and pinches? An elephant wearing a tight tuxedo!' Once the laughter died down, he adds, 'You see, friends, it's easier for an elephant to get into a dinner jacket than it is for a rich man to get into heaven.'[2]

The paradox of rejoicing

In good times, it's easy to be joyful. If we are honest, it's even possible to be happy when bad things happen to other people. By this, I simply mean we may be glad something bad didn't happen to us. But what about when something dreadful does happen to us? It is precisely when we are hard-pressed and challenged that we should rejoice. St Paul meant it when he wrote: 'Rejoice in the Lord always; again I will say, rejoice.' The most obvious question is why would people want to rejoice when they fail? Paul teaches that rejoicing in bad circumstances – combined with prayer – releases God's power to comfort us in our affliction. Here is the rest of the verse:

> Let all men know your forbearance. The Lord is at hand. Have no anxiety about anything, but in everything by prayer and supplication with thanksgiving let your requests be made known to God. And the peace of God, which passes all understanding, will keep your hearts and your minds in Christ Jesus (Philippians 4:4-7).

Paul is warning us not to react emotionally to hard circumstances. I believe that as a culture we have become used to instant emotional gratification – in health, wealth, and personal happiness, so much so, that we lack the faith to believe that, given time, God is capable of working in all circumstances for our good. Therefore, we allow troublesome circumstances to rob us of the peace that passes all understanding. But Christians may look past outward circumstances, 'for we walk by faith, not by sight' (2 Corinthians 7).

Let go and let God

Of course, this principle is a hard one to grasp, and it takes time and practice before we can come to the place where we can trust God when the outward evidence looks hopeless. Nevertheless, God may be trusted.

There is a story of a man who was walking along a cliff-top path. Slipping on dewy grass, he plunged over the sheer chalk face and only managed to save himself by grabbing onto a root. As he hung on he realised in a matter of minutes he would lose his grip and die. In desperation, he called out,

'God if you are up there, won't you please help me?'

Incredibly, a deep voice thundered from somewhere above. 'I am here, my son.'

'God? Is that *really* you?' he said.

'Yes.'

'Then, please help me. I don't want to die!'

'I will help you, my son. Just let go of that root.'

The man peered down at the jagged boulders and the foaming surf 200 metres below. Then he quickly looked back up towards the voice. After several moments, he called out, 'Um, is there anyone *else* up there?' Although this story is far fetched, we must fully grasp that God's ways are not our ways. Yet we have the testimony of many saints who should inspire us to trust God and rejoice in all circumstances.

Consider Mary and Joseph, the parents of Jesus. If they acted on outward appearances, then Jesus might never have been born to the House of David as had been predicted by the prophets.

God promised Mary that although she was a virgin, she would be the mother of the Messiah. Despite any incredulity, Mary cast aside her doubts and was filled with expectation.

In first-century Judea, marriage was not as we know it. Instead of choosing your own spouse for romantic reasons, a spouse was selected for you by your parents. This means that entire clans entered into a betrothal much like a modern corporate merger.

At about age 21, Joseph was the son of a serious and hard-working carpenter with an established business. Mary's father was a poor man. He would have had to work hard to convince Joseph's father, Jacob, that his son should marry Mary, a teenage girl with no dowry. Probably because Mary was well-liked and known for her piety, Jacob agreed and a wedding contract was made. Soon, however, weighty problems pressed in on the newly engaged couple.

They began when Mary told Joseph she was expecting a baby. Matthew tells us that her Joseph suspected that her pregnancy was the result of an illicit love affair. Most people today do not appreciate the stigma in that day attached to adultery. Not only was it considered inappropriate behaviour, it was a capital offence. This means that according to the law, if Joseph publicly accused Mary of adultery, and there was sufficient evidence to support the allegation, she would be hauled to the town dump and stoned to death there, leaving both families forever disgraced.

Joseph was on the brink of quietly breaking off their relationship when an angel told him in a dream that he should marry his pregnant betrothed (Matthew 1:18-25). To his credit, he agreed, thereby ignoring their outward circumstances.

Once this hiccup was sorted out, they were married. One might have expected Joseph and Mary's financial circumstances to take a turn for the better as a reward for their faith and as a preparation for Jesus' royal birth. After all, no one would expect the King of kings to be born in a humble carpenter's house. And, of course, Jesus wasn't born in Joseph's modest house. The child was born in a smelly stable during a period of extended poverty and homelessness for Joseph and Mary.

Next, King Herod, fearful of a new king, placed a bounty on their son's life, and the little family became fugitives. Not much is known about Joseph during Jesus' childhood, but we do know that the faithful carpenter died never having the satisfaction of seeing the fulfilment of the promise that Jesus was really the Messiah. That's faith.

And what happened to Mary? All we know about her is she was a poor widow. To cap a lifetime of hardship, when Mary's special son was 33, Jesus was betrayed by his friends, convicted of a trumped-up crime, and sentenced to die before Mary's horrified eyes. Her son the Messiah was killed like a common criminal. You couldn't blame Mary if she had called out in anguish, 'Is there anybody *else* up there?' But she didn't. Despite all the heartache, she rejoiced, having faith in a good God whom she could trust. And what has been the legacy of her faith? The greatest cause for celebration in history: the resurrection of her son on the first Easter.

You may be suffering now as the result of some failure in your life. But if you are faithful, you will live to see joy, peace, and happiness in your life. God guarantees it. As the prophet wrote, 'Blessed is the man who trusts in the Lord, whose trust is the Lord' (Jeremiah 17:7). What does the word blessed mean? Here are only a few synonyms: joyous, happy, content, glad, rapt and grateful. Despite a hard life, Mary was certainly all of these and more because, believing God at his word, she rejoiced in all circumstances.

The paradox of praise as spiritual warfare

In addition to rejoicing in all circumstances, we are instructed to praise God as well. Praise, like rejoicing, changes hard circumstances. Paul and Silas were in Philippi during a particularly low point in the second missionary tour (Acts 16). Paul had cast a demon of divination out of a young slave who had been exploited and used as a soothsayer by her master (16-18). When the owner saw that the girl no longer was able to tell fortunes, he had Paul and Silas arrested, beaten, and thrown into a stinking dungeon (23-24). The missionaries were shackled to the walls, unable to move, even to relieve themselves when nature called! I don't know about you, but if this had happened to me, I would have been close to being out of my mind with anguish. Paul and Silas probably were, too. But notice what they do:

> Around midnight, Paul and Silas were praying and singing hymns to God, and the other prisoners were listening. Suddenly, there was a great earthquake, and the prison was shaken to its foundations. All the doors flew open, and the chains of every prisoner fell off! (25-26, NLT)

Anyone who thinks that these men were singing because they were happy about what had happened to them is missing the point. The pair had learned that in hardship and failure, praise is a spiritual weapon that unleashes the power of God. In the next verse we see that power in action: '. . . and suddenly there was a great earthquake, so that the foundations of the prison were shaken; and immediately all the doors were opened and everyone's fetters were unfastened' (Acts 16:26). Later we see that the prison guard and his whole family were converted (30-32). Of course, none of this would have happened had the apostles given in to despair!

Many Christians say such miracles never happen.[3] Moreover, they say that such teaching about the power of praise is nonsense. On the contrary: Consider the case of Margy Mayfield.

Stephen Morin was a murderer on the run in San Antonio, Texas. Needing a hostage to use as a bargaining chip, he abducted 40-year-old Margy Mayfield in a car park. Morin threatened to kill Margy unless she sat quietly as he drove her car to the next city. Once the pair was in Margy's car, she heard the Lord say, 'Tell this man I love him.' At the time, Margy didn't know that Morin was on the FBI's Ten

Most-wanted List, and that an hour before, he had savagely murdered a young woman in her home.

Kidnap victim Margy began to tell Stephen about Jesus. She explained to him that if he were the only man on earth, Jesus would still have died on the cross for Morin's sins. Margy had a Christian praise tape in the car, and without asking permission, she played it and praised God in her heart for what he might do. The two listened in silence. Gradually, tears welled up in Morin's eyes. By the end of the day, Margy led Morin to faith in Christ and he turned himself in to the police.[4] A potential tragedy had turned into a blessing because a Texas woman knew about the power of praising God in all circumstances.

Another good example of the power of praise may be seen in God's deliverance of Jehoshaphat's army during a battle at a place called Tekoa. Notice that the praise team precedes the infantry:[5]

> And when (Jehoshaphat) had taken counsel with the people, he appointed those who were to sing to the Lord and praise him in holy array, as they went before the army, and say, 'Give thanks to the Lord, for his steadfast love endures for ever.'
>
> And when they began to sing and praise, the Lord set an ambush against the men of Ammon, Moab, and Mount Se'ir, who had come against Judah, so that they were routed.
>
> For the men of Ammon and Moab rose against the inhabitants of Mount Se'ir, destroying them utterly, and when they had made an end of the inhabitants of Se'ir, they all helped to destroy one another (2 Chronicles 20:21-23).

The same point is made in Psalm 18:3: 'I call upon the Lord, who is worthy to be praised, and I am saved from my enemies.' And also Psalm 84:4: 'Blessed are those who dwell in thy house, ever singing thy praise!' These are but only a few of the hundreds of scriptures that call us to be in a perpetual state of praise. If you have access to the Internet, click on to www.biblegateway.com and do a word check on praise and its synonyms, or get a good Bible concordance and look them up. You will be amazed at what you find.

All things really do work together for good

Few modern Christians have grasped the power of praise to unleash the authority we have as children of God. That's why when our plans fail, we must resist the temptation to take exception. God may have a different plan for our lives.

Therefore, the best response to failure is to praise God, not *for* the failure *(neurotic heresy!)* but for what God is *about* to do in your life *(the manifestation of his power and glory!)* Grateful praise is the key to unlocking heavenly powers most of us only dream of. This is why Paul teaches us to 'rejoice in the Lord always; again I say rejoice. Have no anxiety about anything, but in everything by prayer and supplication with thanksgiving let your requests be known to God' (Philippians 4:4, 6).

This promise dovetails with Jesus' words in John 15:7: 'But if you stay joined to me and my words remain in you, you may ask any request you like, and it will be granted!' (NLT). This is a promise: when we praise God in all circumstances, we can expect to see evidence that God is working in our lives.

When Jesus made this promise, he wasn't describing a 'name-it-and-claim-it' prosperity gospel. Far from it. He was saying troubles lie ahead. When they come, turn to me in praise and thanksgiving. This was to teach us that God is more interested in developing a trusting, loving relationship with his people than he is in merely giving us whatever we ask for.

One minister put it this way: 'If your problems are long-standing, try kneeling.'

Write it down so you don't forget!

I already mentioned that I enjoy going through my old journals. When I do, forgotten episodes return, such as this one from 1988 when I worked for the BBC. The entry simply reads: 'Today I met the film star Julie Christie.' She came in the studio with my colleague who introduced us. A petite woman in faded jeans and a sweater, I thought this striking 47-year-old woman was a student on placement from a university. Miss Christie asked about my work as a religious producer. As she left the studio, she said sincerely, 'Good luck, Mike.' Somehow Julie Christie had managed to make me feel as if it was she who had just met a celebrity!

I'm glad I kept up with my journals, because they remind me that when the Lord calls us to a task, he also enables – no matter how long and frustrating the process may seem. For example, one 1984 entry was made on the same morning I'd been rejected for a job as a newspaper reporter – the latest in a string of recent rejections. I stopped at an ice-cream shop to cheer myself up.

Licking my chocolate cone, I overheard the shank of a conversation between a bald-headed old man and a very worried looking boy of about 19. The old man whispered, 'I'll put it on the prayer list. Don't worry.' With that, the man produced a wad of dog-eared index cards and a stubby yellow pencil and scribbled something down.

After the boy had gone, I lost no time in introducing myself, hoping he might offer to pray for me, too. After some awkward small-talk, I said, 'I heard you tell that boy that you would . . .' I felt my face flush bright red. 'That I'd pray for him?' he offered.

Tongue-tied, I nodded. Now that I was close to this man, I noticed his rumpled white flares and grubby Carnaby Street-style jacket. His knees were frayed and he was missing a few teeth. I wondered if I'd made a mistake by thinking this odd man could help me. 'Oh, I pray for a lot of people,' he assured me. 'The name's Bob.' Mercifully, despite his appearance, he was quite sane.

Bob had been a missionary for most of his life. After his health suddenly declined, he reluctantly returned home and found convalescing not to his taste. He had a small pension and no commitments, so when he was well enough, he told God he wanted to be used for Kingdom work again. Gradually, Bob began meeting people around town and getting to know them.

'Nearly everyone I meet has a need,' he told me. 'So I offer to pray for them.' He pulled out his index cards. The wad was as thick as a club sandwich. 'I make notes of their needs, and then I go back to my room and spend the rest of the day on my knees praying through these,' he said, tapping a blunt forefinger on the cards. 'Time spent in prayer is never time wasted.'

That day, Bob put my name on his prayer list. I'd like to say that I immediately found a job, but in fact, I didn't – not until two years later. By then, my wife and I had moved back to England where we prepared for the birth of our first baby. Meanwhile I endured more fruitless searching for media work at the ripe old age of 32 – an age considered 'past it' in most media industries.

One day, I saw an ad in the *Church Times* for a radio

producer job. Two weeks later, the job was mine. Later, thanks to editors Tony Collins, Wallace Boulton, and Frank Entwhistle, I became an author. My media career had begun years after I had first been called to it, but my journal helped me stay the course, as it still does today.

A journal is a valuable tool. The prophet Habakkuk said when you hear God speaking to you: 'Write down the revelation . . . For the revelation awaits an appointed time. It speaks of the end and will not prove false. Though it linger, wait for it; it will certainly come and will not delay' (Habakkuk 2:2-3).

'When God picked us Jews to be his chosen people,' Woody Allen once quipped, 'why didn't he pick on someone his own size?' Indeed, the history of the Jewish race is one of heroic failure – consider the generations of enslavement in ancient Egypt, the complete destruction of Jerusalem by Rome in AD 70, the pogroms perpetrated by Christians and Muslims during the Middle Ages, the Holocaust, and the current troubles in Israel today.

From the Jewish perspective, Woody Allen's point is not lost. But from God's perspective, Israel has been greatly used, and he has even greater plans for Israel's future.[6] That is why God directed Moses and others to write down the particulars of God's covenant with his people. Without the written word, the Jews might well have dissolved into obscurity like the scores of other ethnic groups that were contemporaries of ancient Israel.

As we try to serve Jesus let nothing stand in our way – not poverty, not age, not infirmity, unemployment – and certainly not our failures. If you take time to write down what God is saying to you on a daily basis, you will remember what God has promised.

Arguably, such written accounts feature much failure. But true joy is reserved for those who have suffered; true laughter comes only from those who have wept bitter tears. If this is so, then success comes only after having tried and failed. James puts it this way: 'Count it all joy, my brethren, when you meet various trials, for you know that the testing of your faith produces steadfastness. And let steadfastness have its full effect, that you may be perfect and complete, lacking in nothing' (James 1:2-3).

Try this one at home

I challenge you to get into the habit of praising God. Psychologists say that it takes 21 days to one month to form a habit. Beginning today, praise God when something goes wrong. Don't worry about your feelings. The average person's feelings fluctuate thousands of times each day, so feelings are an unreliable yardstick of reality. Exercise your will. Your feelings will catch up. But remember, you need to form a habit. Praise God in all circumstance, and see him work powerfully in your life and the lives of people around you. In Chapter 7, more paradoxes: I'll tell you about the man who can claim to be both the greatest failure as well as the greatest public servant in American political history. I'll also introduce you to a failed missionary whose downfall made him a success. Meantime, oughtn't you to nip out to buy yourself a journal?

1. Reported in opinion.telegraph.co.uk, Tuesday, 25 December 2001.

2. I am aware that there are a growing number of churches that are replacing traditional worship services with entertainment. They claim that old-fashioned preaching no longer speaks to post-modern men and women.

They compare their super-large congregations to the small congregations of traditional churches and claim this is the proof that they are right. I have some sympathy for this argument, but we are missing the point if we forget that our job is not to make people happy. Our job is to make people sorry for their sins and to lead them to repent and surrender totally to God. Joy will be a by-product of such a conversion. The best use of humour, therefore, would be humour that confronts people with the Word of God.

3. Thinking themselves rational, they argue that God does not intervene in human affairs in ways such as these. How can these sceptics call themselves Christian and still uphold the creeds? Our creeds actually say that the Roman government killed a first-century rabbi. Yet he was seen alive and well. Moreover, for the next several weeks the rabbi, now claiming to be God himself, was seen by five hundred reliable eyewitnesses, many of whom spoke to him, ate with him, and touched his body. At least one of them, Thomas, flatly refused to believe until he had seen for himself and examined the wounds (Acts 1:3; 1 Corinthians 15:8; Galatians 1:2; Acts 9:3-8; 1 Corinthians 15:6; John 20:24-29). Then, this same former dead rabbi floated off the surface of the earth on a cloud, promising to come back (Mark 16:19; Luke 24:50-51; Acts 1:9-11). How can a person say he is a Christian and yet argue that miracles do not happen? The simple answer must be that they are humanists speaking a Christian language.

4. Source 'Focus on the Family' ministry tape.

5. Jehoshaphat is confident that God has heard his proclamation, so he encourages his people to praise God vigorously for his victory as if they had already achieved it. This principle is seen again and again in scripture, but most especially in the 'Lord's Prayer' where praise is the opening exhortation: 'hallowed be thy name . . .'. (Luke 11:2-4). Moreover, this is why some traditions add praise at the end of the prayer – 'for Thine is the Kingdom, and the power, and the glory, for ever and ever, Amen.' The greatest hindrance to praying and praising in this way is unbelief (see Matthew 21:22 and James 1:6-8).

6. See Romans 11, especially 11:25.

CHAPTER SEVEN

Sowing and reaping

For 28 years Abraham Lincoln experienced one failure after another. In 1833 he had a nervous breakdown. When he ran for Speaker of the House in 1838, he was defeated. In 1848 he lost renomination to Congress and was rejected for land officer in 1849. These failures didn't stop him from battling on. In 1854 he was defeated for the Senate. Two years later he lost the nomination for vice-president and was again defeated for the Senate in 1858. Yet, despite it all, in 1860 he was elected president and went down in history as one of America's greatest presidents.[1]

It is the fear of failure, not failure that cripples people says author Dick Innes. A committed Christian, Lincoln remained true to his calling as a public servant despite his many failures. It is a good thing, too, because his final act as president was to oversee the abolition of slavery in America. His example teaches us that genuine success isn't the absence of failure. It is having the determination never to quit despite many setbacks. Almost every person who has achieved anything worthwhile with his or her life has not only experienced failure but also experienced it many times.

Not what I expected

The inventor Henry Ford once said, 'Whether or not you think a thing is true, you're probably right.' This is an important idea, for often what we think affects whether we become a success or a failure. This was the message of a man named Nick.

Nick came to speak to my church one Sunday. He spoke about not jumping to conclusions about whether or not you are a failure. To make his point, he told this story about his parents who were missionaries to Africa. Here it is as I recall it.

His parents felt called to a church-planting project in a small village in Kenya in the late 1940s. First, they secured permission from the local chief to settle near the main encampment. Soon they bought a small patch of land, built a hut, and without any of the modern tools, they set about farming and trading with the villagers. Nick, being the first white baby these Africans had ever seen, was quite a novelty. His mother was never in need of a babysitter!

After five years, Nick's family had learned the local language, and although they did not try to make converts, they had succeeded in capturing the interest of the old chief of the tribe. He wanted to know why a family of whites would want to settle among his people in a remote part of the world. Nick's father knew that the best possible answer would be an honest one: 'We came because our God directed our footsteps here.'

This reply made a great deal of sense to the chief, and at his request, Nick's father was invited to build a chapel and conduct services in the African dialect. This way, the people could hear and decide for themselves what kind of God Nick's father worshipped. In the next five years, six tribesmen made commitments to Jesus – and one of them was the son of the chief. Before long, more and more people began coming to the church services until, finally, the chief himself came one Sunday, solemnly proclaiming, 'I have seen a change in too many of my people!' Nick's father held his breath, thinking the chief was offended by the changes taking place among his tribe. 'And if worshipping your God can make *good* people better, then I, too, wish to know more about this Jesus from the East.' You can imagine the celebrations that took place in that village that day!

Now, if the story had ended here, Nick's parents would have thought themselves to be successful. But there is more. Shortly after this, Nick's parents were laid low by a serious illness. There were no medical facilities in that part of Kenya then, so all church activities ground to a halt as the two missionaries languished. Some of the tribesmen took this opportunity to point out that the old gods were punishing the missionaries for leading the people away from their traditional religion. Nick's father grieved deeply that he was too ill to refute the gloomy pronouncements of the unbelievers. He had to lie helpless in his sickbed as one after another of his converts went back to their former beliefs. Mustering all the faith they had, the two missionaries began to pray that they would be healed so they could carry on the good work that they had begun.

Gradually it became clear that if they remained in the village much longer, Nick's parents would surely die. After 12 years of toiling, the heartbroken missionaries abandoned their project as a failure, feeling utterly dejected and angry at God's seeming indifference to their prayers.

Nick's story illustrates a point we must never lose sight of as Christians: that just because we are carrying out God's will in the way he has called us, we are not protected from failure – especially failure caused by natural circumstances such as sickness and death.

Certainly miracles do occur, but it's wrong for us to

demand that God intervene in our lives in an extraordinary manner. That is, we must not seek miracles as a convenient means of escaping our sorrows or failures. In my own life, I have experienced many miracles. Two of the most remarkable are that I have been healed of debilitating allergies and my eyes were healed so that I no longer need to wear glasses. (Glory to God!) Yet, I am ashamed to admit that frequently I find myself trying to manipulate God to do *my* will not *his.* It's a case of the clay telling the potter what he may or may not do with his clay (Romans 9:21).

From Africa with love

Frankly, I don't blame Nick's parents for being upset. They poured 12 years of their lives into a project that, on the brink of success, seemed to have fallen flat on its face. What made this all the more galling was Nick's father could see his converts falling back into pagan practice despite having made earlier professions to Christ. In the end, the missionaries returned home like a couple of shattered china dolls. Anyone who can endure that without turning to God and shaking both fists in rage is certainly a strong person. Nick said his father remained bitter and went to his grave a sick and angry old man.

While it is natural to grieve over apparent failures, or to vent our frustration, letting God know our feelings, we must take great care not to lapse into self-pity and morbid introspection because resentment – and ultimately sin – grows up between God and us. The apostle Paul could have indulged in self-pity because of the thorn in his flesh. But it would have brought his ministry to a halt. Instead, he made the best of a bad situation, turning his sickness into an object lesson on spirituality to help fledgling Christians understand more about God's nature (2 Corinthians 12:7-10).

Let's return to Nick's story. Years later, Nick was back in East Africa on business. By chance, he and his colleagues found themselves within a day's drive to Nick's childhood village. So Nick and his friends decided to pay a visit.

Nick supposed the place would be changed. In his childhood, the village had been relatively untouched by the West. Now the children would probably be wearing designer clothes and listening to Walkmans. There would be computers, television and satellite communication. However, the last thing Nick expected to see was any evidence of his late father's church work.

When Nick arrived, it was as he had thought. There was now a paved road, wells, and the bush had been cleared to make way for corn and wheat crops. There were the expected Western additions, including a few purpose-built brick buildings – but to Nick's utter amazement, one of them was a church!

While Nick was there, his childhood friends greeted him. They shared a meal with him, and the pastor of the church was one of the guests. After the meal was ended, the pastor said, 'I came specifically to meet the son of the man who brought the Good News to a dying village!' Nick sat in stunned silence. 'After your family left us,' the pastor said, 'quite naturally the church fell on hard times. But before the work was completely lost, one of the first men your father baptised took over as pastor. It was sad that your family had gone away, but under this man's leadership, the church was not only saved but it grew.'

Nick said that in order for the church to grow, his parents had to relinquish their hold on it. This was God's plan for reaching the lost souls beyond the village. What a reminder to us that God's ways are not our ways (Isaiah 55:8). Tragically,

Nick's father saw himself as a failure. He could not accept that God had intended him to be like John the Baptist – to sow the seed – then to stand aside, allowing others to reap the harvest.

Nick's story has helped me to deal with my numerous failures. Often apparent failures lead to a greater good if we have eyes to see it. We must resist the temptation to be our own judge and jury regarding our failures. Fortunately God is capable of drawing a straight line with a crooked stick. He is the God of new beginnings. No matter how bleak we think our circumstance, we hold on to God's promise: 'Behold, I am doing a new thing; now it springs forth, do you not perceive it? I will make a way in the wilderness and rivers in the desert' (Isaiah 43:19).

Remember that the path to success must pass through the dark alleys and threatening byways of failure. There is a price to pay when we set out to follow God. Think of Noah withstanding the ridicule of his neighbours as he spent vast sums of his money and long days of labour constructing a mighty seafaring vessel hundreds of miles inland. Consider Moses' deep humiliation when God promised him that he was to deliver his people from bondage, and under Moses, the Jews stumbled through a barren desert for four decades, leaving thousands behind in unmarked graves. Nevertheless, God's will was ultimately done. If Noah and Moses knew the agony of defeat why should we be spared?

When the Bible characters seem too remote

When I find that I can't relate well to remote biblical characters, I seek out older men and women whom I know and respect. I am always inspired by their stories of how God was with them when they seemed to fail.

Mary told me that she and her husband had committed themselves to serving God when they got married. They agreed they wanted to have a practical ministry, not just one of worship and prayer, important as that is. One morning, Mary's husband left for work but never came home. In a letter, he said he didn't love her any more, and he wanted a divorce. The hardship of living as a single woman forced Mary to cry out to God to provide the things her husband had always provided. At first, she had to accept the charity of friends. Soon, though, she became more independent. Mary told me, 'There were times when I was sure I was about to go under through lack of money, through a lack of material possessions, but it never happened.

'I kept after God, telling him my needs, and he kept me going with the aid of my church, sometimes with the aid of strangers. I lived one day at a time.'

Many thoughts come to my mind about Mary. Two of the hardest are these: why did Mary's marriage fall apart, and what happened as the result of her telling God that she wanted to serve him? I can't answer the first one, but the second one I can.

I have a newspaper clipping that features Mary. It tells of her efforts a few years ago to raise support to aid victims of a severe drought in Africa. During a BBC radio interview, I asked her how she managed to find the money and a vehicle to deliver food, tools, and other aid that came pouring in to her appeal. She pointed out that since God had proved he was able to provide for her needs after her marriage failed, he could be depended upon to meet other human needs under any circumstances. Since that time, without the benefit of a steady income or the support of a sending agency, Mary has travelled back and forth to Africa, supervising various projects that help villagers improve their living standards.

This is only one of many similar testimonies of older men and women who faced severe trials when they set out to serve the Lord.[2] Ask any older person whom you know and trust. I'm sure many will tell you of heartbreaking failures. Yet it is very likely that they will say that Jesus keeps his promise: 'I will not forsake you nor abandon you.'

Remember, no matter what it feels like now, time will prove that God means what he says and says what he means.

1. Lincoln material by Dick Innes quoted with permission. 'Failure never forever', www.gospelcom.net.
2. This theme is taken up in full in *The Church's Hidden Asset – Empowering the older generation*, Kevin Mayhew, 2001. ISBN: 1 84003 7016.

CHAPTER EIGHT

The origins of failure

For centuries people have been inventing myths in order to cope with reality. Despite their reputation for being pragmatic, embedded deeply in the soul of all Greeks was a nagging longing for the romantic pre-Pandora paradise on earth – when failure did not exist, and there was peace on earth. Can't say I blame them.

Briefly, the ancient Greeks believed that Paradise was lost when a girl called Pandora opened a box and unloosed pain, discomfort, and failure. Two popular ways for the Greeks to cope with these problems were Epicureanism, the philosophy of eat, drink, and be merry today, for tomorrow you die; and Stoicism, the philosophy of enduring pain and discomfort with a passive acceptance.

The Greeks were not alone in their attempts at finding meaning in a short, turbulent existence that ended in destruction. The ancient Hebrews concocted a bilious philosophy of life, springing forth from the writer of Ecclesiastes. Commenting on the utter futility of life, he complains, 'I have seen everything that is done under the sun; and behold, all is vanity and a striving after wind. What is crooked cannot be made straight, and what is lacking cannot be numbered' (Ecclesiastes 1:14-15).

With the dawning of the Christian age, however, this

pessimism gave way to hope thanks to the resurrection of the body. 'Blessed be the God and Father of our Lord Jesus Christ! By his great mercy we have been born anew to a living hope through the resurrection of Jesus Christ from the dead' (1 Peter 1:3).

At last, men and women could be assured of a better life to follow this one. Admittedly, among many other religions, there was a concept of an afterlife, but that place was usually reserved for royalty and other worthies. On the whole, women, children, the infirm, the weak, slaves – the perceived *losers* of those cultures – were not welcome in paradise.

Christian missionaries, on the other hand, went abroad and taught that all are welcome. In fact, Jesus himself taught that the afterlife was more for the poor of this life than the rich masters whom they served on earth (Luke 16:19-31). Why? Because the next life is not bought, inherited, or earned. It is a free gift from God to all that will accept it: 'For the wages of sin is death, but the free gift of God is eternal life in Christ Jesus our Lord' (Romans 6:23). That's why the Christians called it the *gospel* (good news)!

However, for many millions, human suffering, pain and death remained too great a problem. A doctrine that asked a person to wait for the next life for happiness was called 'pie in the sky by and by'. So people continued to look for answers outside the Church.

In modern times, when the so-called New World had been discovered, rumours spread like honey that America was an unspoiled paradise. Spanish sailors told tales of a place in Florida they called El Dorado, a city of gold where everyone was rich and happy and healthy. There was supposed to be a fountain of youth there so you could enjoy your prosperity for ever and never grow old and die. We ought not to scoff at these myths. Today our culture brims with similar claims for products that replace lost hair or make us skinny, operations to make us seem youthful, medications to make us sexy, and escapist entertainment that makes us believe that we are the masters of our universe. This is merely humanity's age-old attempt at coping with a life of fleeting joys, much pain, and the ultimate failure – death. As the sombre preacher of Ecclesiastes moans, 'There is nothing new under the sun' (1:9).

Why is life so difficult?

Something has gone terribly wrong in the world. But what's caused it? The Bible says it was the Fall of Adam and Eve (Genesis 3). The Fall forced men to earn their living by tilling cursed soil all the days of their lives (Genesis 3:17-19).

So many people have trivialised the part of Genesis that tells of the origins of the human race, preferring the Theory of Evolution, which scientifically proclaims that humanity evolved from lower life forms. Adam and Eve is mere religion. But did you know the Theory of Evolution is also a religion?

The religion of evolution

The Theory of Evolution claims humans evolved from apes. Where did apes come from? Earlier animals that evolved out of a primordial protein soup. And that soup came from matter which is formed out of atoms. And where did atoms come from? Ultimately, you have two choices: either A. Atoms always existed, having *no beginning and no ending;* or B. Atoms *created themselves.* If this sounds vaguely like religion, it is. Religion is defined by the *Oxford Concise Dictionary* as: Human recognition of superhuman controlling power, especially God. In place of God, however, evolutionists have made Nature the controlling power (note they even capitalise the N in nature, and ascribe god-like powers to it when they say, 'Nature intended for so and so or such and such'; or 'Nature provided this or that', etc.).[1]

Like any religion, the Theory of Evolution adheres to a faith creed. This creed states that everything was created out of nothing and is somehow evolving towards perfection with each passing decade. I find this somewhat optimistic in the light of our blighted history. Someone once defined an optimist like this: A man fell off the observatory deck of the Empire State Building. As he hurtled toward certain death, a reporter stuck his head out of a window on the fiftieth floor and shouted, 'How does this experience feel?' The man chuckled, 'It's great, *so far.*' That's an optimist. You have to be like this fellow if you think the overall quality of life is improving with each passing year. The Theory of Evolution has its holy books – known as textbooks. In a typical textbook, you will see an artist's impression of evolution illustrated by a parade of animals beginning on the left with a single-cell creature, to a fish-like creature, progressing through to hairy bipeds, and ending on the right with a modern man striding boldly towards evolutionary perfection. Evolutionists have proved none of this, so the Theory of Evolution is a faith doctrine, and its claims must be understood in the light of its creed.[2]

The religion of the Bible

According to the Bible, God, not Nature, always existed. He designed and created everything in the universe. Humanity was created perfect and designed to live for ever in harmony with the rest of creation. However, Adam's sin shattered the *status quo*, causing the mayhem and failure we know today. Moreover, according to the Bible, far from evolving towards perfection, humanity is on a downward spiral, which after a short life of pain and sorrow, terminates in death, the ultimate failure. It is not my purpose to try to prove or disprove the existence of a literal Adam and Eve, but we have only the story of the Fall if we hope to understand the Christian origins of failure. Whichever religion we prefer to subscribe to – Evolution or Biblical Creation[3] – each requires great faith to believe it.

What the apostle Paul says

Paul alludes to Adam and Eve in the forum at Mars Hill in Athens where he appeals to the Greeks' liberal-mindedness in order to teach them about Jesus. In addition to their own pantheon of gods, they had a shrine dedicated to the 'unknown god'. Paul points out to the Athenians, 'you have been worshipping [the unknown God] . . . without knowing who he is, and now I wish to tell you about him. He made the world and everything in it, and since he is Lord of heaven and earth, he doesn't live in man-made temples; and human hands can't minister to his needs – for he has no needs!' (Acts 17:23-25 *Living Bible*).

Here we see Paul the iconoclast. He runs the risk of insulting the Greeks by rebutting one of their time-honoured myths, that their gods actually live in man-made temples.

In his letter to the church in Rome, Paul identifies the origins of all human failure: 'When Adam sinned, sin entered the entire human race. His sin spread death throughout the world, so everything began to grow old and die, for all sinned (Romans 15:12, *Living Bible*). It's pretty plain, then. The origin of failure comes from our separation from God through sin.

Failure: the price of free will

Eve and then Adam ate a piece of fruit. They really shouldn't have eaten it, but they did. Yet, is that any reason for God to slam the gates of Eden in their faces, turning them out into a cursed world to endure harsh failure? What parent would react that strongly if a child disobeyed what seemed to be a trivial rule? We need to examine the facts of this case carefully before we attempt to answer these questions. According to Genesis 2, Eve and Adam were quite happy in their relationship with God and obeyed his wish that they don't eat the fruit of a certain tree in the centre of the garden. At the start of Genesis 3, however, a snake (Satan) creeps into the garden and confuses Eve. He tells Eve that God has lied to her. If she eats the fruit, she will not die. She will instantly be like God and know good from evil (Genesis 3:1-5).

Satan, the original liar, mixes in some truth to muddle Eve's thinking. The lie is that she will not die; the truth is that her eyes will be opened to awesome knowledge. Satan has planted doubts about God's nature in Eve's mind. She must exercise her free will. She has to decide if God, whom she knows intimately, is trustworthy. She reaches out and grasps the fruit and holds it. Satan's lies cause her to doubt God and to feel dissatisfied with her life. She wants to be equal to God.

Fanning the flame of pride is Satan's speciality. Pride, after all, is what caused Satan to fall from heaven (Revelation 7:9; Luke 10:18). Ever since then, Satan has been working to overthrow God's purposes in the universe by enticing humans to rebel. Eve began to covet God's knowledge and power, and to anticipate gaining exclusive knowledge and self-sufficiency. Satan must have held his breath, watching with maddening expectancy to see if his victim would bite into the fruit of her own free will. The evil one knew that until she did, she was still under God's blessing because dissatisfaction and pride are merely *potential* sins in the form of temptation.

Temptation alone is merely the overture to sin which is why Jesus taught us to pray 'lead us not into temptation' – Matthew 16:13. To illustrate, I'd like to tell you about my friend Tom. He and his wife once found some *Penthouse* magazines under their son Gary's mattress while they were changing the bedding. They were very embarrassed by the pornographic pictures. Removing the material, Tom decided to wait for the right moment to talk to his son about the magazines.

After dinner Tom invited Gary into his study for a cup of coffee. After chatting for a while, he gently confronted Gary, saying that he and his wife had accidentally found the magazines. There was an awkward silence. Then Tom explained, 'Gary, your mother and I strongly disapprove of the way sex is depicted in those magazines. I think you know why.' The teen nodded sullenly. 'To demonstrate our disapproval, I have no choice but to punish you for bringing these into our home.'

What Tom did next drives home an important point about sin as opposed to mere temptation. 'Before I send you to your room, Gary, I want you to know something else. After I found those magazines, I came down here to think about what I was going to do about it.'

The boy nodded, now hardly meeting his father's eyes.

Reaching out and touching the boy's shoulder, Tom swallowed hard and said, 'I want you to know that I was very tempted to close the door and sit in here and enjoy looking at those pictures myself.'

Gary glanced up sharply and looked in wonder at his father who continued. 'There's nothing wrong with having an appetite for the opposite sex. I enjoy making love to your mother, but this stuff is degrading not only to the men and women who pose for the pictures, but it degrades a wonderful gift given to us by God, the gift of intimate sexuality. God understands our appetites, but he also expects us to be strong enough to stand firm when they tempt us to sin. It isn't easy, I know – but I wanted to show you it can be done.'

James puts it this way: Resist the devil and he will run from you (4:7). According to the accounts in Genesis 3:1-6, after hearing Satan's lie, instead of resisting and turning away, Eve was convinced. She exercised free will and the result was the first human failure in history. A little later, Adam ate the fruit and the tendency to sin was begun.

God created sin?

A few years ago I was commuting back and forth to work near Philadelphia. One day I saw some graffiti painted in broad white strokes on a wall by the side of the road. It read, 'God Created Deseas' [sic]. I smiled at the spelling and promptly forgot about it. The next morning as I drove to work, I saw that someone had taken white paint and below the first message had added the words, 'An' all de fishes in dem'.

Ignoring the 'Philly' accent, the idea that God created disease and therefore sin, suffering, and failure, while terribly misguided is hardly new. Although he wilfully ate the fruit given to him by Eve, Adam tried to cover his responsibility by accusing God of the ultimate blame, saying: 'But it was the woman *you* gave me who brought me some, and I ate it' (Genesis 3:12, *Living Bible*, italics mine). As if the Lord was responsible for abusing the gift of free will!

Consequences of Adam's sin

The Judaeo-Christian explanation of how death and every sort of evil entered into the world may be traced back to Adam and Eve's sin (Genesis 3:17-18). Their reign in Eden depended upon their desire to obey God. Adam and Eve made a choice. They disregarded God's warning not to eat the fruit. Wilful disobedience brought spiritual and physical death into history. None of this was God's intention, but Adam and Eve gained forbidden knowledge of good and evil, which meant from then on, they and their offspring were culpable.

Jesus – the one and only second chance

If the Bible spoke only about the origins and effects of human misery, then this Adamic story would be no better than the Pandora story. However, the Bible formulates an exceedingly important doctrine, using the sin of Adam as the kernel of the argument. Paul declares that where Adam failed, Jesus did not. Jesus was the world's only perfect human being:

> What a contrast between Adam and Christ, who was yet to come! And what a difference between our sin and God's generous gift of forgiveness. For this one man, Adam, brought death to many through his sin. But this other man, Jesus Christ, brought forgiveness to many through God's bountiful gift. And the result of God's gracious gift is very different from the result of that one man's sin. For Adam's sin led to condemnation, but we have the free gift of being accepted by God, even though we are guilty of many sins (Romans 5:15-16, *Living Bible*).

Paul mentions the name of Adam several times in his discourse. This means that the account of the Fall is of central importance to Christian doctrine since it explains where human failure comes from.[4] Secondly, although we continue to fail, oftentimes dismally, there is reason to be optimistic because of the hope offered to us through Christ.

God weeps

As did Jesus Christ, we all must endure failures that leave us scarred. But when we are scarred by failures in our attempts to serve God, we must not forget that Jesus stands with us in every trial. When we weep, he weeps. What choices we make will affect whether we fail or succeed; however, God will not remove our right to choose, for by so doing, he terminates our humanity, reducing us to puppets which he controls. Still, we can know for certain that when our choices lead to grief and pain, God stands beside us and provides a way forward. This is what Paul means when he proclaims that we are not to be hostages of Satan in our failure-prone universe. Consider the following four liberating promises found in Romans 8:14-17:

1. For all who are led by the Spirit of God are sons of God.

2. For you did not receive the spirit of slavery to fall back into fear, but you have received the spirit of sonship.

3. When we cry, 'Abba! Father!' it is the Spirit himself bearing witness with our spirit that we are children of God.

4. And if we are children, then we are heirs of God and fellow heirs with Christ, provided we suffer with him in order that we may also be glorified with him.

Remember, God has not called us to be successful; he

has called us to be faithful. In the next two chapters, I will be putting Moses and Peter in the dock to investigate their failures. I hope to show that God can use our failures to bring about a greater good if we allow him. After all, this is the essence of Christian faith: that all things are working together towards the consummation of history in the victorious return of Jesus Christ. Meantime, we must remember that Satan is always waiting to pounce on us like a lion, so we must stand firm when he attacks (1 Peter 5:9).

1. There is a newly minted 'C' choice being bandied around by certain evolutionists who finally recognise that classical evolution is pure religion. They say that primitive life did not originate on earth at all. Rather potential life was carried here as spores on ancient meteorites. When the meteorites crashed into the earth, their chemicals merged with existing chemicals to produce the building blocks of life. Of course, this still begs the question about the ultimate origin of atomic matter.

2. For an in-depth treatment of this subject from a secular point of view, see *The Facts of Life – Shattering the Myths of Darwinism* by Richard Milton, Corgi Books, 1993. The *Times* said of Milton's book that it could shake the religion of Darwinism as much as *Honest to God* shook popular religion 30 years ago. For an excellent series on science written from a Christian point of view, see United Christian Broadcasters' 'Evidence for Truth' series. For details, ring 0845 60 40 401, or write to: UCB Direct, Mulberry House, Chelmsford Road, High Ongar, Essex, CM5 9NL.

3. For a fuller explanation of Scientific Creationism from a Christian perspective check out this website: http://www.scientificcreationism.org/

4. Significantly, if Adam and Eve and the doctrine of Original Sin are removed from Christian belief, there remains no need for Jesus to die on a cross to pay for our sins. Briefly, Original Sin is the belief that through Adam, we inherit his guilt at birth. This tenet is first expressed in Psalm 51:5 and carried through into the New Testament. While there are some variations about how Original Sin is to be understood, there is no doubt that we all are affected by it.

CHAPTER NINE

The fugitive

A wealthy young man sees a member of his own gang being beaten up by a hated rival. In a frenzy, he searches through his pockets, keeping his eyes fixed on the scene before him. At last, his eager fingers find what they are looking for. Charging into the fray, his trembling hand flies into the air and there is a blinding silver flash of a dagger against the cloudless blue sky. Next comes the rip of splitting threads and the sickening tear of human flesh.

There is an astonished groan. The limp body falls with its full weight to the ground and twitches. A river of blood seeps into the cracks of the dry earth and excited blowflies buzz out of nowhere to lay their eggs in the gaping wound. 'Run! He'll never raise his hand against any of *us* again!' cries the young man with the dagger.

After the boy he has just rescued has sprinted away, he wipes the wet dagger on the dead man's sleeve. The young man sheaths the weapon, then hides the body in a sandy grave. When he is done, he walks calmly away, certain that no one has seen his crime. Yet in less than 24 hours, he will be a fugitive, running for his life into a future as an abject failure.

Sound like a scene from an old James Dean film? Perhaps it's an updated version of *Romeo and Juliet* from the revolving stage at Stratford upon Avon, and young Romeo is on his way to his only friend, Friar Laurence, in search of safe-keeping? Actually, the young man is Moses, and this was to be the first of many colossal blunders made by one of the Bible's greatest saints (Exodus 2:11-15).

Moses now had a police record. Having had the opportunity to write extensively about criminals, I can say without fear of contradiction that the lowest caste in any society, the person most likely to have the word *failure* stamped on their forehead, is the man or woman who has a police record. I found this out first-hand a few years ago when I was doing research at HM Prison, Exeter.

In spite of the bright blue sky and the intense sunshine, the massive Victorian buildings before me drained me of all my early morning cheerfulness. I removed my rucksack and craned my neck left and right, unsure of how one gains entrance into Exeter Prison. Seeing a narrow road to my right, I made a false start, finding my path fenced off. Retracing my steps, I spied a woman carrying her shopping. I noticed that as she approached me, she kept her eyes straight ahead.

'Excuse me, please,' I said, smiling. Not batting an eyelid, the woman walked on as if she didn't hear me. 'Madam . . .?' She increased her pace. Because I was standing with a ruck-sack outside a large prison, she evidently thought I was a just-released ex-convict. Insulted by this cold treatment, I shrugged and walked on.

Former convict Billy McFetridge tasted the discrimination the hard way. He was once a lieutenant in the UDA, a Protestant paramilitary organisation. He went to prison on multiple charges under the Prevention of Terrorism Act in 1981. After a remarkable conversion behind bars, he became an exemplary prisoner and left prison 12 years later to attend Bible College. Since the early 1990s, he has been involved in a successful Christian prison ministry that reaches out to prisoners and their families. His story is told in *Prisoner of Hope* (New Wine Press, 1998).

A few years ago, Prison Fellowship International founder, Charles Colson, invited Billy to visit the United States to honour this prison reformer for his work in the United Kingdom. While filling out his visa application, Billy was asked if he had ever been arrested. Indicating that he had, he completed the form and sent it off. Not long after, he received a crisp letter saying that his application to visit the USA had been denied because of his prison record. Billy's work as a qualified prison worker, his credentials as a minister, and the support of several leading Catholic and Protestant Christian leaders meant nothing in the light of his having once been in jail. To this day, the American State Department considers Billy to be *persona non grata* in the USA.

Once someone has been branded as a criminal, they must either live with that stigma for life, or try by whatever means possible to run from the past. One of several reasons why few criminals are truly reformed after having been to prison is that society does not believe they have reformed. Criminals are perceived as permanent social failures.

In his autobiography *Killing Time*, Noel Fellows – a man accused and imprisoned unjustly for manslaughter – experiences these problems acutely after being released from prison. Like Billy's, his life is now a testimony to God's goodness, but he feels no less strongly the injustices that were inflicted upon him both during his prison sentence and afterwards when he tried desperately to build a new life against the odds society mercilessly threw at him.

Moses the criminal

Moses had been the adopted grandson of the all-powerful Pharaoh. Now he was a criminal on the run. He made his way into the only place left for him to go – the desert. Keeping the facts about his crime under wraps, he began a new life in the far-off land of Midian. There this once-heir to the throne of Egypt was grateful for the lowly job of herding a flock of sheep for a priest named Jethro.

The life of a shepherd is a quiet one, and Moses would have plenty of time to mull over his past. Thinking about his crime, he would have seen that while his intention was noble – he was trying to protect a helpless Hebrew slave from the cutting whip of an Egyptian overlord – his method was wrong. By killing the Egyptian, Moses had broken the law.

One day, his wanderings brought him to the mountain of Horeb, or Mount Sinai, a barren and inhospitable land. 'If only I hadn't killed that man,' he might have said bitterly through gritted teeth. (He wouldn't have worried who heard him since only sheep surrounded him!) 'If I hadn't, I could have helped my people by using my position in Pharaoh's household. If I go back to Egypt now, I'll be arrested and killed.'

Apparently someone else was listening. No sooner had Moses spoken than he met with the Angel of Jehovah who appeared in the form of a burning bush (Exodus 3:2-9). No doubt Moses was at once terrified by the mysterious voice, yet at the same time overjoyed by the good news that at last his people were soon to be liberated. As he stood trembling with excitement, Moses wondered how God planned to free the Hebrews, though he did not ask. He had too much respect for the power and majesty before him. Knowing his thoughts, though, his question was answered: 'I am going to send you to Pharaoh, to demand that he let you lead my people out of Egypt' (Exodus 3:10).

Reeling at this piece of absurd news, Moses replied, 'But I'm the wrong man for that job!' (Exodus 3:11).

With God all things are possible

Why would God select a man who is branded by society as a failure to undertake so momentous a task? Surely, when someone wants an important job done, he selects the best person for the job. If I needed to have an audit done, I would not pick an accountant who appeared to be incompetent, let alone one whom I knew was a criminal. However, that would be judging the person purely by outward circumstance. God, on the other hand, sees beyond outward circumstances.

Moses did not know of Jehovah's compassion towards sinful failures at that time. He was about to enter into a powerful learning curve. Meantime, he was faced with the awesome prospect of having to return to Egypt where he was wanted by the law. From one point of view, this is rich comedy. An outlaw is confronted on a barren mountaintop by a talking bush, which although it is on fire, is neither hot nor being consumed by the flames. What's more, this bush is telling Moses to go back to the last place on earth he dares show his face. If it were a film, you could imagine Woody Allen cast as Moses, complete with his owlish horn-rimmed glasses and New York Accent: 'Oi vay! They won't listen to a *schlemiel* like me!' (Exodus 4:1).

To assure Moses that he needn't worry, God promises to do miracles to establish Moses' credibility in the eyes of the Hebrews and Pharaoh. That's when Moses points out another of his failures – he has a speech impediment. I can hear Woody Allen say, 'Anyway, I can't go back there. I'm allergic to death!' (Exodus 4:10).

As Moses and the bush stand there arguing, one thing becomes perfectly clear. Moses is not the confident, natural leader we often imagine him to be. In fact, the longer this dialogue goes on, the more unsuited to the task Moses seems to be. This drives home a key point that God wants to make to people everywhere: none of us, in our own strength, is capable of serving God properly. Humanly speaking, all of us are failures before God's standard. J. John, Steve Chalke, John Stott, Billy Graham, Pope John Paul, Derek Prince, or Moses himself – all have sinned and fallen short of the Glory of God (Romans 3:23).

Regarding Moses' speech impediment, God replies frankly that since it is he who makes mouths, Moses' mouth is no problem (Exodus 4:11). Since this is so, we needn't worry about our failings when it comes to serving God. This point merits some unpacking. One of the tricks Satan loves to use is based on his understanding of the concept of our self-image. Moses' humility is in fact self-pity, the opposite of genuine humility. Since God is not relying on human talent to carry out his work, any that wish to serve him needn't feel inadequate to the task, no matter what their limitations are. In fact, the more severe the human limitations, quite often, the more powerfully they are used by God. Only we must be willing to do God's will – he won't force us.

It takes a special kind of grace to say, 'Here I am, God; use me – just as I am.' People who are not afraid to speak to God this way find there is no end of important tasks needing our attention. I heard a story about a remarkable old woman that lived in Moscow when Christian books were contraband. Soviet churches were desperate to receive Christian books from the West that were very hard to come by. When one or two got past the officials, the only way the material could be distributed was by making typed copies in the Russian language and handing them around to cell groups. The KGB was quick to figure out where the illegal printing operation was housed, and so such operations were routinely closed down with the leaders put in jail.

One day an elderly woman volunteered to head an operation from her tiny flat. 'I will type up the books,' she offered. The leaders eyed her: she was literally bent double with arthritis and bound to a wheelchair. Her mottled hands were twisted, and her digits looked more like a bird's talons than fingers. 'But how can you type the books, Mother?' one of them asked kindly. The old woman extended her pointer finger and wiggled it. 'I can use this,' she said, grinning.

Reluctantly, they agreed to move the operation to her tower block. Slowly but surely, one manuscript after another was produced by her labour of love – pecking away with one good finger. As the books began to make the rounds of Moscow, the KGB went into a frenzy to discover who was running the illegal press. More than once, her building was thoroughly searched, but since the police knew she was a poor old widow crippled with arthritis, they never bothered to search her flat. And so the books continued to be typed out.

God in you

There is a small parallel between Moses' feelings of inadequacy and an experience in my own life. When I started producing programmes for the BBC in Oxford, it was on a six-month trial basis. To be honest, I felt entirely unequal to the task. First of all, the job was religious producer. My predecessor had been ordained, and I wasn't. Second, the lion's share of my journalism experience was in print media, not broadcasting. Scared of the prospect of a colossal failure live on air, I began to wish I hadn't got the job! When I told my wife how I felt, she pointed out, 'You're the one who told God he could use you any way he saw fit, right?' I nodded peevishly because I knew what she was driving at. 'So your attitude is pretty bad. I think you owe it to God to assume that if he wants you to have this job, then you will be able to do it. After all, you won't be alone. God will be with you. Meantime, if you don't start thinking pretty seriously about what you intend to produce, you'll have nobody but yourself to blame if you do mess things up!'

Of course, I knew she was right (as usual), and that I was simply looking for excuses which would compensate for the hurt I might feel if I was given the sack after my trial period. What was worse, though, was I was acting as if I did not believe that God had a plan for my life.

Some Christians say that we can't know for sure that God has a plan for our lives. Their argument comes down to this: do we act out of our own free will, or are we merely actors playing our roles directed by God? Both beliefs have strong arguments supporting them. But I believe that God is in control of all the events of our lives. Jeremiah 29:11 states, 'For I know the plans I have for you. . . . They are plans for good and not for evil, to give you a future and a hope.' Some Christians go so far as to say that God reserves parking places for them. I don't know about that, but I do know that when we place our lives entirely in Christ's hands, God is fully in control. In fact, we are not having our free will subordinated. Our will is to do God's will; our desire is for God to be in all we say and do.

At any rate, Moses was positive he could not accomplish the tasks God had set before him. When he at last simply begged God to spare him from such grand plans, rather than torture his faithless servant, God made special arrangements to help Moses get started on the road to faith. He allowed Aaron and Moses to work together, supporting each other. Aaron was to speak, and Moses was to give his brother the words to say (Exodus 4:14-16).

Let my people go!

Travelling back to Egypt with Aaron, Moses was able to convince the Hebrews, with the help of Aaron, that God had indeed selected them to deliver them from slavery. This was no easy piece of persuasion. Some of the people who had heard of Moses would have known him as a murderer that ran from Egyptian justice. Yet the majority of the people recognised God in Moses and knew he was to be their only hope of salvation.

Moses knew he was no longer in danger in Egypt because the reigning Pharaoh was not the same one who reigned when Moses committed his crime. Moses and Aaron were granted an audience with the ruler of Egypt and requested in the name of the God of Israel that the Hebrews be freed and allowed to leave the country (Exodus 5:1).

The task of convincing the closed-minded Pharaoh was not easy. For one thing, Egypt's mighty economy depended on the free labour provided by its Jewish slaves. But Exodus chapters 5-12 portray Moses as a man of great patience and skill when it came to dealing with the stubborn whims of the Pharaoh. Moses was discovering that the more he trusted God, the more God proved his faithfulness. But faith always precedes performance!

Moses found that for a servant of God to complain about the daunting task of trying to do God's will would be like a ship's captain complaining about the sea, to paraphrase Enoch Powell. That's why it came as no real surprise when the exasperated Pharaoh finally said, 'Leave us; please go away, all of you! Go and serve your God!' (Exodus 12:31).

This was surely Moses' finest hour because Moses became an overnight superstar in the eyes of his people. To this day, Jews celebrate Passover to commemorate the departure of their ancestors from slavery into freedom, a thing every Jew cherishes above all else.

God – the author of history

If this story had been a screenplay written in Hollywood, it would have ended with the Jews marching boldly out into the sunrise, singing a jubilant pop song while the film's credits rolled up the giant screen. But the truth is, Moses' adventures were only just beginning. He was destined for some pretty trying times in the years ahead in the wilderness. The time Moses spent tending Jethro's flocks were not wasted. Just as sheep can be fickle, stubborn, and stupid, so were God's chosen people.

Once the Hebrews reached the Red Sea the honeymoon was over. Pharaoh had changed his mind and was in hot pursuit, intending to retrieve the people he considered to be his own personal property. Of course, the Hebrews wouldn't be fearful. They had seen Moses perform miracles. They saw the plagues. They could still see God's burning column in the sky, the promise that God was with them (Exodus 13:22).

Nevertheless, with an almost united voice, they turned on their stunned leader:

. . . and they said to Moses, 'Is it because there are no graves in Egypt that you have taken us away to die in the wilderness? What have you done to us, in bringing us out of Egypt? Is not this what we said to you in Egypt, "Let us alone and let us serve the Egyptians"? For it would have been better for us to serve the Egyptians than to die in the wilderness' (Exodus 14:11-12).

How different are we today? I don't know about you, but I have a very bad habit of forgetting the times God has helped me through difficulties the moment a new disaster strikes. Most of us err on the side of pessimism rather than optimism during severe trials and various failures. When the Egyptians came in sight and the Hebrews criticised Moses, I am sure he must have felt like throwing himself in the sea.

If Moses had opted for suicide, this story would be nothing more than a profoundly pessimistic tale, like many of today's novels. Fortunately the author of human history is not a Booker Prize winner. God is the God of optimism. He always offers us a way out.

Another reason why Moses did not really despair was he had seen God get him out of other tight spots, and he was prepared to believe God had not led them into the desert to allow Pharaoh to recapture them. I often wish I could have been there to see Moses confidently say to his people, 'Don't panic! You are about to see the power of the God we serve.' Moses would have paused and looked hard at the marauding Egyptian army, adding, 'By the way, take a good look at that lot because in a few seconds from now, they are going to die' (Exodus 14:13). Moses raised his arms, and immediately God sent a strong east wind that caused the sea to part, allowing the future nation of Israel to escape. After the Egyptians rode into the dry passageway, the waters suddenly crashed closed and every man and horse was drowned (Exodus 14:21-28).

In the wilderness

Like a computer program virus, the Hebrews began to grumble on the east side of the Red Sea when food and water ran short. Once again, Moses said, 'I can assure you that there is nothing I can do for you. But our God can!' The very next morning, and every day for about forty years, the children of Israel had manna – a white gum like coriander seed and bdellium with a honey taste. They found the food on the ground fresh each morning like a delivery from a heavenly Domino's Pizza.

For the time being, Moses had regained the respect of his people. Soon, however, this man of God led the Hebrews into the wilderness at Rephidim, a kind of Death Valley and Sahara Desert rolled into one. At about the time Moses realised his mistake, the people called out in one peevish voice, 'Give us water!' Some of the people were so unimpressed with Moses' navigational skills that they wanted to stone him. By this time Moses had to be thinking of stepping down from his God-appointed role. After all, under his watch, a relatively straightforward fifteen-day procession was turning into the march from hell. Panic set in and Moses forgot his original agreement with the Lord which stated clearly that it would be God not Moses who would be in complete control of the exodus. So when God told Moses to strike the rock and that water would gush forth, Moses felt great relief. Sure enough, there was water enough for all (Exodus 17:5-6).

Not as easy as it looks

On one hand, it looks as if Moses had it easy. Each time he

failed, all he had to do was call on God and, hey presto, a miracle was provided. The reality, however, is much different. For one thing, Moses was required to call on God in humble, child-like faith because God is not our servant. Proof that Moses was in the midst of some kind of deep faith crisis can be seen in an account of the exodus in Numbers:

> And Moses said to the Lord, 'Why are you treating me, your servant, so miserably? What did I do to deserve the burden of a people like this? Are they my children? Am I their father? Is that why you have told me to carry them in my arms – like a nurse carries a baby – to the land you swore to give their ancestors? . . . They keep complaining . . . I can't carry all these people by myself! The load is far too heavy! I'd rather you killed me than treat me like this. Please spare me this misery!' (Numbers 11:11-12; 14-15 NLT)

This clearly is a man who has been crushed by his responsibilities and his failures. You may be sure that many Christians – especially clergy – often feel this way, too.

Moses' heart was in the right place, however. He actually loved his people and he didn't want to see them destroyed. He also knew he didn't have the option of declaring himself mentally bankrupt. Although he was probably seriously tempted to, he couldn't simply stay in his tent one morning, saying, 'Sorry chaps. I can't be bothered any more. I'm at the end of my tether. You'll just have to find your own way without me.'

In the midst of these serious setbacks, Moses knew the way forward was not on his feet but on his knees. He fell on his face and begged God to have mercy on him and on the very people who were condemning him as a miserable failure.

Sometimes people fail because other people have plotted against them. The Hebrews were calling for Moses to step aside. Young David failed many times in his bid to become his people's anointed king because the reigning monarch, Saul, used all his energy and might to frustrate David. Still, David would not hit back at Saul. (See 1 Samuel 24:8-11.)

Here is an important lesson to us all. Both men had to forgive and even pray for their enemies before God would act on their behalf. The Lord looked on Moses' heart and gave him the strength to carry on loving these stubborn and fickle Hebrews.

It only hurts when I grow

Sure, following God is easy. All you have to do is invite Jesus into your heart and then be willing to die for your faith. Actually, following God in twenty-first-century Britain is a darn sight easier than it was for poor Moses. Few, if any of us, will ever be called upon to bear the staggering responsibility faced by Moses. Yet hard times make us the people God wants us to be. In Moses' case, failure made him depend more on God and less on himself. We would do well to allow our failures to have the same effect on us.

Often we want to stay inside our comfort zones where all is safe and predictable; but with each test we face comes a learned lesson, a new skill, a greater ability which proves to be valuable later on. As one fitness instructor I know often says, 'It only hurts when you grow!'

Make us a god!

Moses considered his worst failure to have occurred while he was high up on the summit of Mount Sinai conferring with God. While he was away, he appointed Aaron to be his deputy. Before long, the Hebrews grumbled that Moses had been away too long. Next, they began to question God's existence despite all that they had seen with their own eyes. (This is why I never take seriously people's statement, 'If I see a miracle, then I'll believe.' Remember, it's not a case of seeing is believing; rather, it's believing is seeing!) Next, the Hebrews persuaded Aaron, a talented goldsmith, to forge them a golden calf so they could worship it in the mistaken belief that the calf and not almighty Jehovah had led them safely out of Egypt.

While Moses was on the mountain, God told him what his people were up to and threatened to destroy them there and then. Moses pleaded for the misguided and sinful Hebrews and the Lord relented.

Moses scrambled down the mountain, but when he got there, he was not prepared for the perverted scene before him. Not only did the Hebrews go chasing after a false god, but also they were caught up in a sacrilegious orgy of sex, booze and perversion the likes of which Moses had never seen. He exploded in a fit of pique and lashed out at his brother. Deciding a tongue-lashing was not enough, he commanded the priests and men of the tribe of Levi to kill 3000 idol-worshipers.

This harsh punishment may be difficult for us to understand, but what Moses did the next day helps us to see that the sins were very serious indeed. Note what Moses suggests to God:

> So Moses returned to the Lord and said, 'Alas, these people have committed a terrible sin. They have made gods of gold for themselves. But now, please forgive their sin – and if not, then blot me out of the record you are keeping [God, don't kill them, kill me instead!]' (Exodus 32:31-32, NLT).

Moses' willingness to sacrifice himself out of love for his sinful people not only shows how the agony of his failure matured him, but it is also a clear foreshadowing of the love sacrifice Christ was to make for us, his equally sinful people.

I'm no saint!

Often I hear people excuse their failures by saying, 'I'm no saint.' They must have a distorted idea of what a saint is supposed to be like. You and I are saints according to St Paul (1 Corinthians 6:2; Ephesians 2:19). But as saints, we may lose our jobs, create strife, become jealous, and even sin against God. In other words, we are just like people who do not profess to any faith at all.

Moses, the murderer and the failed statesman, was a saint and a sinner. Certainly Moses' greatest sin was when he struck the rock with his staff. At that time, there was an acute lack of water, and the Hebrews were, as usual, in a mutinous mood. Sensibly, Moses and Aaron fell on their faces and prayed. God heard them and said to take the rod and go to a certain rock and tell it to pour forth water. Relieved, they jumped to their feet and gathered the people, promising that they shall have water. This time Moses seems to have quite forgotten that it was God, not he, who provided for our needs.

> And Moses and Aaron gathered the assembly together before the rock, and he said to them, 'Hear now, you rebels; shall we bring forth water for you out of this rock?' And Moses lifted up his hand and struck the rock with his rod twice; and water came forth abundantly, and the congregation drank, and their cattle (Numbers 20:10-11).

Ostensibly, Moses did as God told him to do, but note the hint of pride in Moses' words. Remember that Moses was ordered to speak to the rock. Instead, Moses struck the rock because he was angry at his people whom he called 'rebels'. His scathing comment, 'Do we have to bring you water from this rock?' indicates a tone of self-importance and a distinct lack of love for his fellow refugees. Whether this is a simple lapse in judgement or a wilful decision to disobey God is not for us to say. What happens next, however, sheds clear light on how God regarded this behaviour. 'And the Lord said to Moses and Aaron, "Because you did not believe in me, to sanctify me in the eyes of the people of Israel, therefore you shall not bring this assembly into the land which I have given them"' (Numbers 20:12).

So after forty years of hard labour and all the severe lessons he had learned, Moses, the great law giver, the man who spoke face to face with the Almighty and lived, the deliverer of the whole nation, was not allowed to set foot in the Promised land because of this single act.

We may think that this is harsh punishment for something as benign as hitting a rock twice. After all, previously, Moses murdered a man, and God didn't punish him for that. Likewise, when he first met God in the form of the burning bush, Moses defied the Lord, yet God remained fatherly, albeit, firm. So why this sudden change of attitude on God's part? Remember that God sees what the human eye cannot see. Moses' previous failings were not motivated by pride. Motive is what counts with God. For whatever reason, Moses became inflated with his own self-importance. This prompted him suddenly to look down on his brothers and sisters, perhaps fancying that he was better than they. God will not tolerate this attitude in his children. Paul teaches, 'Do nothing from selfishness or conceit, but in humility count others better than yourselves' (Philippians 2:3). With God, it is not the sin as much as the intention that is important.

After all, weren't Adam and Eve evicted from Eden for eating a piece of fruit? Hardly! They were puffed up with pride, and like Moses, this failure cost them dearly.

A father's love

The true measure of Moses character must be gauged at the end of his life. Moses composed a song of praise to God whom he had served for the last forty years of his life. Then, despite the ultimate failure – that of being denied the honour of leading his people into the Promised Land – he blessed each of the tribes in turn and then spoke of God. This older and wiser man said:

> 'O Lord, the God of the spirits of all living things, please appoint a new leader for the community. Give them someone who will lead them into battle, so the people of the Lord will not be like sheep without a shepherd' (Numbers 27:15-17, NLT).

Are these the words of an unrepentant and failed leader? Are they bitter, resentful words like those of the failed presidential hopeful, Richard Nixon, who in 1960 scathingly said of his defeat, 'You won't have me to kick around any more'? No. These are the loving words of a kindly father more concerned for the welfare of his wayward children than for the colossal loss in his own life.

The lessons of failure

At the beginning of this chapter, Moses was a fugitive outlaw. Even if he had been captured and sent to prison for his crime, it is unlikely that Moses would have been reformed, as prisons are notorious for making bad people worse. But after God came into Moses' life, his failures and disadvantages were gradually turned into blessings and advantages.

In the eyes of the world, Moses may be considered a consummate failure. Called by God to lead the Hebrews out of slavery into a Promised Land, Moses wandered aimlessly in the desert for forty years. However, the most crushing failure came at the end of Moses life when he and the Hebrews were within sight of the Promised Land. At this crucial moment, God refused to allow Moses the honour of leading his people into their future homeland. God selected Joshua, a much younger man to succeed Moses. If anyone had the right to be bitter, it was Moses. However, despite the outward appearance of failure, he continued to trust and obey.

Joshua went on to be a great leader of the Hebrews. Why? Partly because of natural gifting. But in a much more realistic sense, he had learned from seeing Moses' failures.

This is an important point. Joshua saw Moses' flaws and shortcomings, yet he never forgot that Moses worshipped God in good times and in bad. For Joshua, Moses was a role model for how he must act when facing conflict and failure.

We lose out on important training if we try to shield ourselves from life's painful moments. That is the humbling lesson of failure, but as Peter wrote, 'So humble yourselves under the mighty power of God, and in his good time he will honour you' (1 Peter 5:6, NLT). Peter ought to know.

We heard so much about foot and mouth disease a few years ago. Well, Peter knew about foot *in* mouth disease, as we will see in the next chapter.

CHAPTER 10

Man of passion

Dawn is breaking. A silent figure steals along narrow back-streets in a large Middle-eastern city. He wears a heavy woollen cloak, hitched high on his neck to obscure his familiar profile. In his fevered mind, every bump, every footstep means he's surely being followed.

At the shrill yowl of a cat, the man dodges down an alley, breaking into a canter until at last he reaches his secret destination. There he frantically taps on the door then pauses. In the agonising seconds that pass, a curse catches in his throat. Growling, he now pounds his fist on the door, grazing his hairy knuckles on the rough oak door.

At last a timid voice from within calls, 'What do you want?'

'Open up, you fool. It's me!' he whispers through clenched teeth.

An iron bolt slams back and the door opens to reveal a gaunt man with a thick brown beard. The red rims and dark semi-circles under his eyes show he hasn't slept that night, and his lined face is the colour of a flounder's belly.

'Peter, where have you –?'

Grabbing James by his bony shoulders, Peter cuts off the question. 'This time I've really failed the Master,' he wailed. 'Do you hear me?'

'I've failed him, too. Remember, I was in the Garden when they took him away.'

'No, for God's sake! It's worse than that, James! Not an hour ago, I was with him at the house of the high priest.'

A look of hope crosses James' face. 'Did you speak up in his defence?'

Peter buries his face in his large callused hands and cries, 'No. I denied even knowing him, three times, just when my testimony might have helped the Master. *Three* times!' Peter's baritone suddenly boomed into the frosty air, 'I denied him once for each year I knew him.'

James' eyes widened in terror. Taking Peter by the arm, the younger man pulls him inside, scolding, 'Will you pipe down, you old fool. Do you want the centurions to find us?' With that, the door slams shut and the bolt rasps back in place.

Why me, Lord?

When our performance is so unspeakably bad it disgusts even us, it's very tempting to give up – just as Peter did after Christ was arrested and accused of crimes he never committed. Since even knowing Jesus would have been suicide, who could blame Peter for failing to acknowledge his relationship with the Lord? (Matthew 26:69-75).

On reflection, though, it's surprising that Jesus selected Peter among the twelve apostles to be the leader of the first church considering this craven act of betrayal (Luke 22:31-32). It was not the first time Peter failed his Lord. And it wasn't to be the last time, either. To be sure, the other apostles had their fair share of failures – Thomas was a sceptic (Luke 20:24-25); James and John were hungry for glory (Matthew 20:20-28); Nathaniel was a racist (John 1:46); and all had abandoned Jesus at his arrest. However, because the Gospels are so full of Peter, and because Jesus speaks most often to him, let's focus on this flawed man.

Certainly Peter was honoured among all the followers of Christ. For instance, the very first time Jesus came into Peter's home, Peter's mother-in-law was seriously ill and languishing on her deathbed. To everyone's utter delight, Jesus asked to see the woman and healed her of a fever (Luke 4:39). Although in the months that followed, Peter saw Jesus cure other sick people, his mother-in-law's healing must have left a deep and lasting impression on him and his family. Thus it's easy to understand that when Peter subsequently gave up his successful fishing business to follow an itinerant preacher, there was little or no protest from his family, even though they were partners in the business!

Peter was a man bred on the water, and it made sense to him when Jesus said, 'Follow me and I'll make you a fisher of men!' Not long after, however, Jesus and his twelve followers were out in a boat crossing a lake. As the men navigated, Jesus became weary and stretched out in the sun for a nap. But while he was asleep, a squall came up and the wind began to thrash the small sailing craft. Although Luke doesn't mention any names, it's more than likely that it was Peter, the implied leader of the band, who shook Jesus awake, calling, 'Master, Master. We're sinking!'

Christ turned his bearded face into the gale and growled, 'Quiet down!' with the firm authority of a man secure in his power to control the elements. Then turning to the twelve, and no doubt glaring at Peter, Jesus demanded, 'Where is your faith?' Whatever they replied outwardly, inwardly they were filled with dread for Jesus, asking themselves, 'Who in the world is this man that even the wind obeys his commands?' (Luke 8:22-25).

One day in a crowded square, Peter deftly inserted his foot in his mouth after a woman suffering from chronic haemorrhaging touched the hem of Christ's dusty robe, knowing Jesus would heal her. Pivoting, Christ queried, 'Who touched me?'

Peter, who felt more at home on an isolated beach among his nets, was probably agitated by the throng of urbanites milling about Jesus like bees in a hive. He tugged at his beard and exploded, 'Master, there are hundreds of people here to see you!'

Jesus' reply once again put Peter in the dog house. 'No, it was someone who deliberately touched me because I felt power go out from me.' Seconds later, Peter learned that a woman had been healed by her faith in Jesus, although she had been diagnosed as incurable by the best doctors of that day (Luke 8:45-48).

After witnessing Christ's authority time and time again, one might think that Peter would have known better than to question the Master's behaviour. Certainly, Peter had more than an inkling of who Jesus was. After all, it was he who spoke for the twelve when he answered Jesus' question, 'Who do you say I am?' Peter answered correctly when he replied, 'You are the Messiah' (Luke 9:20).

Yet Peter continued to get it wrong. For example, when Jesus decided it was time to explain to the apostles what men would do to him, he referred to the scriptures teaching that the leading religious experts would reject him. He spelled out that he would be arrested, tortured, and finally killed. But, he assured them, he would also rise from the dead three days later (Mark 8:31). This was not new to Peter or the others, for the texts were ancient – Isaiah 52:13; 53:1-12. Yet, Peter clearly missed the point Jesus was making, for he took Jesus aside and reprimand him. It's not hard to imagine the scene: 'Lord. A little while ago you were telling us that you were about to be killed. Did I understand you right?'

'Yes, Peter, you certainly did. My time is short and –'

Grabbing Jesus by the arm, he explodes, 'Hang on a moment, Jesus. If I were you, I'd be careful not to go around saying things like that.' Glancing over his shoulder at the other apostles, he adds, 'You know, some of the lads like John there, or Judas. They're a little sensitive, like. They might not know what you mean. I'm not sure I understand you either.' Puffing out his chest, he continues, 'Anyway, Lord, you got me to look after you so you can go on doing all your miracles and what not. And as long as I'm with you, you'll be safe.'

Looking ruefully at the blank faces of the apostles and then back at Peter who is still preening himself, Jesus spits, 'Satan, get behind me!' Peter twists around but there's no one there but him.

'Who are you calling Satan, Lord? Me?'

'Yes, Peter.' Sighing, Jesus tries to explain. 'You are only seeing this from a human point of view. I'm seeing it from my Father's.'

Imagine Peter's mortification. Yet again he spoke out of turn, and this time he even had to endure Christ calling him *Satan* in front of the others. I'm certain that Peter wanted the earth to open up and swallow him. He may even have begun to think about quietly slipping away and going back to his nets and the sea where life was so much simpler for a crude loudmouth like him. Although no scripture records this, it is easy to see Peter confronting Jesus tearfully, saying, 'You appointed the wrong man to lead the group, Master. Why not make John the leader? You love him and he never seems to get it wrong. Or how about Philip? He's so *reliable*. I'm sure he'll understand you when you talk about these spiritual things.' As always, an ever-lurking demon would be right at Peter's elbow, egging him on and grinning to hear Peter fall for the old trick of comparing himself unfavourably with others.

Still, Jesus would be unmoved. He knew exactly what qualities he wanted when he selected Peter to lead. For all his flaws, Peter had something that God wants in all his leaders. Peter had *passion*.

When you look at the great saints, you will notice two things. All were prone to failure, and all had great enthusiasm in following Christ. Peter was certainly ready to do anything and go anywhere for God. For me, one of the most touching examples of Peter's fidelity to Jesus is recorded in John 6. Here Jesus has told his Jewish disciples that he is the bread of life. Speaking metaphorically, he explains, 'He who eats my flesh and drinks my blood has eternal life, and I will raise him up at the last day' (John 6:54). This was spoken in a synagogue. When he said it, there was an outburst of disagreement. Some said Jesus was a blasphemer. John tells us that that day, Jesus lost a significant number of his followers. When the crowds dwindled to only a handful of disciples, Jesus glanced sadly at the apostles and said, 'Do you also wish to go away?' (67). Peter alone replied, 'Lord, to whom shall we go? You have the words of eternal life; and we have believed, and have come to know that you are the Holy One of God' (68).

While Peter did not have any formal theological training, he did know the truth thanks to John the Baptist. Peter had been a disciple of John during his ministry along the Jordan River. This is what Jesus saw when he looked at Peter: a man of conviction, not a dreamer. He didn't see a failure; he saw a man who one day would organise the first missionary movement, a man who would inspire other saints to dare to attempt great things for the Kingdom, a man who would muster the faith to perform the first of many miracles in the name of Jesus of Nazareth, healing a cripple at the Beautiful Gate of the temple (Acts 3:2-10).

You may be feeling like a failure right now. If so, don't allow Satan to accuse you of the obvious. Remember that God sees us as we can be. This means that to serve God well you don't need a perfect track record (who can claim that, anyway?) If success were a prerequisite, then all of the saints of the Old and New Testament would have been eliminated systematically.

The death of failure

Through plentiful examples, I have aimed to prove that Christians are bound to err, sin, and fail – sometimes miserably – as they attempt to serve God with the gifts and talents God has given us. Whatever the circumstances, we must not lose sight of this fact: We may often lose skirmishes and small battles in this life, but we have already won the war through Jesus Christ our Lord and Saviour. In the eternal sense, we are winners. Romans 8:37 proclaims: 'In all things we are more than conquerors through him who loved us.'

The conflict is won and Jesus is victorious. We may have this assurance even as we look discord squarely in the eye. This is our hope, the one thing that makes Christians the happiest people in the world. As Paul wrote nearly 2000 years ago: '"O death, where is thy victory? O death, where is thy sting?" The sting of death is sin, and the power of sin is the law. But thanks be to God, who gives us the victory through our Lord Jesus Christ' (1 Corinthians 15:55-57).

Christ's Sermon on the Mount makes it clear that being a Christian requires great humility. Let's look at Peter again. The best known incident where he failed to understand the authority we each possess as followers of Christ is the time he saw Christ walking towards his boat across rough seas (Matthew 14:22-23). Peter wanted desperately to show Jesus that he had faith. Peter asked the Lord to call him out of the boat onto the water. When Jesus complied, Peter clambered over the side of the boat and to the amazement of his companions, began to walk on the water towards Jesus. Certainly it was not through Peter's own ability that he accomplished this feat. That he could even have stood on water and not sink is a wonderful object lesson illustrating Mark 10:27 – with God *all* things are possible. Clearly, Peter had managed for one bright and shining moment to demonstrate the awesome power we have as the children of God.

Two men stood on the surface of a rough sea. But I am convinced by what happened next that there was an unwelcome but ever-lurking third person on the waves that day, although Scripture doesn't point him out. It was a demon. And that demon was determined to trip up Peter.

I am aware that many Christians feel that when anyone mentions demons, they may be guilty of ascribing too much power to Satan, who is, after all, a defeated enemy. Defeated or not, he is still a dangerous enemy. Jesus warned Peter of satanic activity in Luke 22:31: 'Satan wants to sift you like wheat'. Later on, Paul and Peter write to other Christians warning them about the powers of darkness that have one goal in mind – to do battle with the Church. Paul states categorically that Christians are up *against powers and principalities* in the spirit realm (Ephesians 6:12-18). Peter writes of demonic attacks, adding that demons are like wild beasts seeking *to devour* naïve Christians (1 Peter 5:8). C. S. Lewis shows clearly in *Screwtape Letters* that Satan is not able to be in two places at one time, so he must depend on a lowerarchy of fallen angels to help him get up to mischief in London and in San Francisco on the same day.[1]

Fortunately, evil spirits and demons do not dominate the spirit world. There are also angels which encamp around the faithful as David wrote in Psalm 34:7. That means if we could picture the unseen realm, we would see a host of spiritual creatures anxiously looking on to see how the Church is doing (Hebrews 12:1; 1 Peter 1:11-12; Ephesians 3:12).

Here is how the demon on the sea might have prompted Peter to stop trusting Jesus and to start trusting in himself:

Demon: Peter, my good man, you're a fisherman and well acquainted with the properties of water and the laws of nature. Don't you know it's impossible for you to, *ahem*, walk on water?

Peter: (To himself) Uh oh! My toes are getting wet. What was I thinking of when I jumped out of that boat?

Demon: Well, you're out here now and all of your mates are looking at you. Whatever happens now, Old Boy, you mustn't blow it. Do hurry up before you begin to sink!

Peter: Good grief, what'll the lads think of me if I muck this up? Maybe I should start to run.

Demon: Jesus will never let you forget it if you blow it again. I tell you what. Have faith in yourself and you can do it.

Peter: I can do it. I *know* I can do it. I – Aaahiii!

But it was too late. Peter's faith wavered, fear set in, and the rest is history. Peter began to sink. 'Help me, Lord,' he sputtered as salt water filled is eyes, nose and mouth. 'I'm drowning!' And once again, Jesus had to criticise passionate Peter for setting out in faith, but then giving in to the human temptation of trying to please God in his own strength.

Peter's problem here is twofold: He initiated a task that Jesus had not asked of him, and then he set out to complete it under his own strength.[2] The result was inundating! Peter's anxiety to succeed created a climate of fear and God cannot or will not honour fear. He honours only that which is undertaken in faith. Romans 14:23 says he who doubts is condemned even before he starts.

Peter also fell for the old sin of humanism or self-actualisation – the belief that we may do anything provided we try hard enough. This is, of course, nonsense, but it has permeated our society through mass education, the media, pop-psychology, and the New Age Movement. Fortunately, Peter called out to Jesus whom he knew and loved. Indeed, it was his passionate love for Jesus that saved his life on that occasion. But note that that love did not prevent Peter from failing; nevertheless, Jesus loved Peter back because the Lord saw something deep inside this man whom he called 'The Rock' (or Rocky, as I like to think of him!)

At the opening of this chapter, we saw Peter during the lowest point of his life – the day he denied Jesus three times. Writing from the comfortable distance of 2000 years, and with the benefit of hindsight, it's tempting to imagine that if I had spent three years in the intimate company of the Messiah, I would have been bold enough to say to Pilate at Jesus' trial: 'You bet I know Jesus. And so do you, you old hypocrite! And I also know he's being framed, so let my pal go!'

Or would I? Actually, I wouldn't bet my life on it.

1. I am not one to use the word 'prophetic' loosely, but having recently reread *Screwtape Letters*, I am certain that Lewis was writing in a prophetic mode, particularly in Letters 8-12. If you have never read *Screwtape Letters*, do so.

2. This was the same error I had made when I was trying to become a missionary. See Chapter 1.

CHAPTER ELEVEN

Rocky II: a shot of reality

I once heard a woman say, 'I can resist anything except temptation.' She was being facetious, of course. But there is a profound truth embedded in her comment. Too often we are overconfident about what we would or would not do in a difficult situation. Bible scholar and author Derek Prince once said that if you think to yourself, 'I would never do that' – be it cheating on your spouse, fiddling your income taxes, telling a lie, or stealing paper clips from work – then you are a candidate for a fall from grace.

In the previous chapter, I painted a picture of myself strutting before the assembled chief priests and elders at Jesus' trial. Shouting for effect, I imagine myself asserting, 'As all of you know, I have been with Jesus constantly these last three years; therefore, my testimony is better than anything you pack of snakes could patch together. I say he is the Messiah!' Of course this bit of bravado is nothing more than a self-flattering flight of fancy. The truth is, if the times I have made mistakes, have chosen not to get involved, or have stood by in frozen indecision while someone else suffered are anything to go by, it is very likely that I, too, would have denied knowing Christ – perhaps even five or six times, not just three!

Better that we humbly admit that we are capable of the

most despicable acts and pray that God would 'deliver us from evil and lead us not into temptation' as Jesus taught us to pray (Luke 11:4).

I'm aware that some may argue that Peter's failures happened to him prior to Pentecost. As the Holy Spirit was not yet upon Peter or the apostles, the argument goes, they were incapable of dealing with the problems Spirit-filled Christians take in their stride. This is a fair argument. The conduct of the bewildered apostles who huddled behind bolted doors and shuttered windows like fugitives from the law contrasts sharply with their fearless behaviour after Pentecost. Suddenly, they came out of hiding and boldly preached Christ crucified and raised from the dead, and they were able to convert thousands (Acts 2:41).

This never could have happened without the help of the Holy Spirit. However, the Holy Spirit is not insurance against failure. To suggest such is foolish indeed. Spirit-filled Christians can and do fail. And we will continue to fail until the resurrection. Paul, speaking well after Pentecost, makes this point very clear. In Romans 7:21-24 he laments:

> When I want to do good, evil is right there with me. For in my inner being I delight in God's law; but I see another law at work in the members of my body, waging war against the law of my mind and making me a prisoner of the law of sin at work within my members. What a wretched man I am! Who will rescue me from this body of death? (NIV)

And in 1 Corinthians 13:12 he concedes:

> For now we see in a mirror dimly, but then face to face. Now I know in part; then I shall understand fully, even as I have been fully understood.

From these two points and a score more like them, we begin to see the reality of what it means to be a Christian.

Being a Christian isn't about being good; it's about putting our faith in Jesus (Acts 10:43). It isn't a guarantee that we will have a life free of failure; it's about having hope in the midst of the conflicts of this life and the certainty of eternal life with Jesus in the next (John 3:16). It isn't about trying not to sin; it's about repenting when we do (Romans 10:9).

This doesn't mean we should excuse our sins, but it does mean we needn't feel guilty when we get it wrong. Guilt is the last thing a Christian needs. After all, the scriptures make it clear that sinners don't see themselves as God sees them. 'For my thoughts are not your thoughts, neither are your ways my ways, says the Lord' (Isaiah 55:8). When guilt is taken to its logical conclusion, grace dies. God doesn't cultivate guilt, he offers hope.

An old bumper sticker proclaimed: 'Christians aren't perfect; they are merely forgiven.' Peter demonstrates well this point in Acts 10:14. Peter's stubbornness is hard to believe. He has a vision from the Lord in which he is ordered to include non-kosher food in his diet. Peter has already been through this all-too-familiar scenario many times in the past, and though he is now filled with the Holy Spirit, he still replies impetuously 'No, Lord! In all of my life, I have never eaten any foods that are unlawful!' This is rich comedy in one sense, for here we see the foul-mouthed fisherman telling God what the law requires of good Jews. Even using a gift of the Holy Spirit, a mental picture, God has to drive home his point again and again. The vision has to be repeated *three* times before Peter would accept that God was ordering him to eat pork, shellfish, and certain kinds of 'unclean' birds (Acts 10:15-16).

Once again, I can identify with poor Peter. Over a decade after receiving the Baptism of the Holy Spirit, I still have some difficulty dealing with certain spiritual gifts, particularly pictures or words of knowledge (1 Corinthians 12:8) given to me for other people or myself.

Businessman Andrew Bird, and wife Helen, were thinking of opening a Christian retreat centre in Suffolk. After several attempts at buying property fell through, they decided to look further afield. One evening they dropped by our home to pray about this matter. As we prayed, I had a series of pictures for Andrew, including visions of a roomy country house set in gently rolling East Anglian landscapes. At first, I wasn't going to say anything, for fear of confusing them about where God wanted them to set up this centre. However, in the end, I told them what I saw and left it at that.

Later, Helen told me, 'One day (not long after we prayed) Andrew came home and said, "I think God has shown me the right place."' Within weeks, they acquired an ancient farmhouse and forsaken fruit farm in the heart of Constable country. Ancient isn't an exaggeration. There is a ruined Roman villa in the middle of their 80-plus acre Suffolk spread, and over the years, different owners collected coins, jewellery and bits of pottery which the Birds now own. Forsaken is apt description, too. The land and farm buildings have been neglected for years. Nevertheless, partly as a result of my picture, Andrew and Helen both say they heard God clearly tell them to buy this spread and stay in Suffolk.

Since it's advantageous to act on pictures and words of knowledge sent to us by the Holy Spirit, what was Peter's problem? The crux of his uncertainty is twofold. Peter is loaded down with a cultural bias against Gentiles, a prejudice so firmly ingrained in his attitude that it affected his personality. He also displays religious pride by presuming to know God's mind better than God does. We shouldn't be too critical of Peter regarding this last point. Ever since the Fall human beings have been making dogmatic assertions about God – and most of the time we have been wrong. Thankfully, God still is willing to forgive us.

Not long ago I came across a book of Christian doctrines. I found much there to be helpful. However, I was astonished to read the section dealing with alcohol consumption. Rather than simply admitting that certain denominations have a cultural bias against drinking anything fermented, it attempted to 'prove' that the wine Jesus created at the wedding feast in Cana was really non-alcoholic grape juice. The so-called logic was as circular as the person who declared, 'I have now borrowed enough money to pay off all my debts.'

Alcohol is not the only thing that causes division among Christians. Many denominations teach that the age of miracles is passed, and that signs and wonders, including the use of tongues, words of knowledge, and other gifts of the Holy Spirit died out centuries ago. I know about this because for the first 19 years following my conversion to Christ, I taught against such things. I regret it, and if I could, I would go back and apologise to each person who tried to teach me about these faith-enhancing gifts.

Deliverance is another can of worms. There is a well-known British writer who seems to have a grudge against this particular ministry. In many of his books, he makes it a point to stigmatise this form of pastoral care. Like Peter and the question of unclean food, he knows better than God. I think we all need to be mindful about what we claim God will or will not do, given our limitations.

Let me make an analogy. We have a border terrier called Buddy. Buddy knows plenty about me. When I reach for my key, he knows to move to the kitchen door so he can be included in my outing. When I am grumpy, he knows to stay out of my way. If I feel sad, he crawls up to my chair and licks my hand.

Buddy knows a lot about me. But when I am thinking about my work, or what I plan to do next year, Buddy can't begin to understand my thoughts. Like Buddy, we can know certain things about God's behaviour and his character, but his thoughts and his deeds are infinitely beyond human understanding. The writer of Proverbs puts it like this: 'A man's steps are ordered by the Lord; how then can man understand his way?' (Proverbs 20:24). Fortunately for us, we live in a day when we have the completed Bible as our roadmap. Peter, on the other hand, did not have the full Bible, so he did the best he could.

Peter's belief that he knew more about God's will concerning kosher food and the apostle's loathing of Gentiles was the first step toward another of his classic pratfalls. This time, however, Peter is saved. Shortly after Peter's word of knowledge, the Roman Centurion Cornelius (a hated Gentile), sends servants to beg Peter to preach the Word so that he can become a follower of Jesus, too. Normally, Peter would not have responded to a non-Jew, let alone accompany one into his home. Yet he agrees.

Although Peter's actions were considered unorthodox, he was, in fact, doing God's will. When he was criticised by other Jewish Christians, he found himself defending Gentile evangelism despite what the law taught about the need to be wholly separate (Acts 10:34-48). Until that time, following Christ was for the Jew only!

My point is this: despite being Spirit-filled, the Church in Jerusalem was pig-ignorant of God's fuller plan of salvation. Peter, and later others, acted as God's spokesmen in order to put God's plan in action (Acts 11:1-18). Peter's action gave the green light to Paul and Barnabas to begin their missionary outreach to the Gentiles (Acts 15:22-29). Had Peter not finally conceded that God was doing a new thing (from his Jewish perspective) no non-Jew would have ever been invited to become a follower of the Jewish Messiah, Jesus Christ.

The right stuff

Let me recap my main point here: Spirit-filled Christians make mistakes and often fail in their feeble attempts at serving God. Peter, with his many egregious failures, is living proof of this fact. So why did Jesus single him out to lead the early Church? Simple. God was peering into Peter's heart and he liked what he saw there.

Jesus' knew Peter was to be his man from their first meeting. Peter was returning from a long and unproductive night on the water. Jesus was waiting to meet him on the shore. When they had been introduced, Jesus tells Peter to go out and try once more to catch some fish. Anyone who has ever worked a night shift will know how annoying this suggestion would sound, particularly when it came from a well-meaning landlubber! Yet here is Peter's reaction recorded in Luke 5:1-8:

> 'Master,' Simon replied, 'we worked hard all last night and didn't catch a thing. But if you say so, we'll try again.' And this time their nets were so full they began to tear! A shout for help brought their partners in the other boat, and soon both boats were filled with fish and on the verge of sinking. (NLT)

I can just see Jesus standing on the shore with his hands on his hips and a smile splitting his face from ear to ear as he watched the fun. When Simon Peter realised what had happened, he fell to his knees before Jesus and said, 'Oh, Lord, please leave me – I'm too much of a sinner to be around you.'

Notice Christ did not respond by saying, 'Oh, er, yes. Now that you mention it, of course, you will have to stop sinning first, and of course, to follow me you must never fail. Once you get yourself sorted out, laddie, give me a ring. Here's my card.' Instead, Jesus was pleased by this development, for he loved the pugnacious fisherman. With a twinkle, he responded to Peter: 'Don't worry, mate. From today on, you'll be fishing for men!' (See Luke 5:10.) This reply to Peter's candid admission typifies the patience Jesus shows towards all that turn to him in passionate contrition after they fail or fall short of their ideals.

Jesus wants passion above all else. Maturation comes in various degrees and at different stages in our lives. Passion is what God first looks for in all of us. The Lord prefers a wholehearted error to a half-hearted attempt at doing what is right. The proof is in Revelation 3:15-16: 'I know all the things you do, that you are neither hot nor cold. I wish you were one or the other! But since you are like lukewarm water, I will spit you out of my mouth!'

As we have seen, despite his passion, Peter still has a talent for failing on a grand scale. His three denials following Jesus' arrest was the supreme failure. After the resurrection, Jesus appears to Peter and asks the dumbfounded apostle three times if he loves him – once for each denial: 'Peter, do you love me?'

'Yes, of course I do.'

'Peter, do you really love me?'

'You know I do, Lord.'

'Peter, do you love me more than these others?'

Peter, embarrassed and shamed by the repeated question retorts, 'You know my heart, Lord. You know I love you!'

To this, Jesus solemnly orders: 'Then feed my sheep.' Jesus was entrusting Peter and the eleven to carry on the work that he had begun (John 21:15-17).

This would not be an easy task, and Jesus wanted Peter to know this. Take special note of the very next thing Jesus says to Peter. He foretells the price that Peter would have to pay by accepting the task – nothing less than death on a cross (John 21:18-19).

Much can be said about Peter, but he may never be described as lukewarm. The evidence lies in his life and the service he rendered to his Lord until he was killed. More than any of the other apostles, including Judas Iscariot, Peter made blunders that could have ruined his chances of serving God. But after each failure, he picked up the pieces of his life like shattered porcelain, learned from his mistakes, and tells all who find themselves in similar circumstances:

> In this you greatly rejoice, though now for a little while you may have had to suffer grief in all kinds of trials. These have come so that your faith – of greater worth than gold, which perishes even though refined by fire – may be proved genuine and may result in praise, glory and honour when Jesus Christ is revealed (1 Peter 1:6-7, NIV).

Coming from a man who failed as much as old Rocky, I think we ought to heed his words.

CHAPTER TWELVE

In God's time and in God's way

People say if God showed them a miracle, then they would believe. This is nothing new. It was the same in Jesus' day.

At Jesus' trial, King Herod hoped to see a miracle, for he, too, had heard of this Jewish rabbi who could raise the dead. Like an eager little boy speaking with a magician, Herod pressed Jesus with question after question, but for Herod and his courtiers, there was no display of signs and wonders (Luke 23:8-9).

When Jesus was taken into custody, a battalion of jaded Roman soldiers packed the room where Jesus was held like punters going to the Saturday match. Expecting a cheap entertainment, they called out for him to demonstrate that he was really a king. When Jesus did not comply, they stripped him and beat him mercilessly with their bare knuckles and tore out clumps of his beard.

After this, he was scourged with a cat-o'-nine-tails – a brutal Roman whip made of leather cords tipped with broken bone, glass, and nails. The beating was severe, gouging Jesus' flesh, and tearing it away until his ribs were exposed in places.

Next someone got the bright idea to throw a scarlet robe over his shoulders. Another used an iron bar to press a crown of razor-sharp thorns into his scalp, sending channels of blood cascading into his eyes, down his lacerated face, and onto the stone floor. If this were not enough, the mob bowed and scraped before their wounded victim in mock adoration, hoping this would goad Jesus into some display of his power. This rough treatment was enough to kill a man, and doubtless, the massive loss of blood would have meant his body was in shock, yet Jesus resisted until they tired of this sport and a centurion led him away to his execution (Mathew 27:27-31).

Even at his crucifixion, people demanded that Jesus show some evidence of his deity. As Jesus hung by the nails that pierced his wrists, scarcely recognisable to his mother and close friends, there was a frenzied atmosphere among the many spectators near his cross. 'Ha!' they shouted. 'Look at you now. You said you could destroy our temple and rebuild it in three days.' Crucifixions were common. Few people if any turned up at these public executions. So why the crowds? What did these people want? One lone voice sheds light on why so many had come to this particular execution. They came to see a wonder: 'If you're really the Messiah, save yourself and come down from the cross! Come down and then we'll believe you!' (Matthew 27:39-42).

It must have been tempting for Jesus to use his power to save himself. After all, he was beside himself with intense pain and anguish. Instead, Jesus remained steadfast in his mission, knowing that signs and wonders were a thing of the past *for the time being*. I'll come back to this point shortly. For now, let's unpack why Jesus had to die in the first place.

Memo from Satan to all devils: Jesus' death must be stopped at all costs!

For years, Satan had been trying to kill Jesus. Following Jesus' birth in Bethlehem, a proclamation was made by King

Herod that all baby boys under age 2 were to be slaughtered (Matthew 2:16). During Jesus' 40-day fast in the desert, Satan appeared to him and tried to get him to commit suicide (Luke 4:9). Later on, more than one priest had ordered that Jesus be stoned to death (John 8:59).

Up to now, all of Satan's attempts to kill Jesus failed. Ironically, just when Satan thought he had got his victim, reality came crashing down upon him with the cold shock of a North Atlantic breaker. Christ could not be killed by him or by the Jews or by the Romans! Far from being the end of Israel's Messiah, the crucifixion was the moment for which Jesus had been sent. Biographer Garry Wills points out that in an early sermon, St Augustine of Hippo said of the crucifixion, *it was a mousetrap with Jesus the bait to trap the devil and thereby end his dominion over mankind.*

Sensing the manoeuvre, the devil suddenly reversed a long-standing order: Jesus must be kept alive at all costs! *Come down from the cross now and we'll believe!* If ever there was a demonically inspired demand, it was this, for Satan was just beginning to understand that he had played right into God's hands by encouraging this crucifixion. Far from being murdered, Jesus was allowing himself to be a sacrifice for sin (John 19:30).

Contrary to what so many people believe about the crucifixion, Jesus was no tragic hero, no victim of mob mentality and contemptible Roman law; he controlled his own destiny, declaring that no one could take away his life. He plainly said that he alone had the power to lay down his life and the power to take it up again – and he was just about to demonstrate this fact (John 10:14-18). His death would demonstrate for all the ages that he was the Son of God (Matthew 27:54). At the same time, it would break

Satan's short-lived rule over the earth. As it is written in Colossians 2:15:

> [His sacrifice] won the victory over powers and rulers. He showed that they had no power at all. He showed the world his victory through the cross (World Wide English translation).[1]

But why must a man *die*?

A well-known philosopher once said that he found Christianity repugnant because it taught that blood was required to appease God's wrath. This attitude is understandable from merely a human point of view, but it demonstrates our gross ignorance of the enormity of sin from God's point of view.

When Adam sinned, humanity became debtors to a holy God (Romans 6:23). For centuries, Jews relied on the blood of animal sacrifices as payment for this debt. The writer of Hebrews explains fully how these blood sacrifices made by human priests were a mere foreshadowing of the ultimate payment which was made by Jesus, the one true sacrifice (Hebrews 9:1-28). At last, it was time to stamp 'paid in full' across an ancient bill that required the blood of a sinless man. Jesus was that man. In reality, Jesus' death was a voluntary act of love done on behalf of fallen humankind, as was his Father's will (John 3:16). This was his mission: 'He died for our sins, just as God our Father planned, in order to rescue us from this evil world in which we live' (Galatians 1:4, NLT).

Jesus would demonstrate his power again three days later at the resurrection (1 Corinthians 15:20). After that, he would oversee the birth of the Church, and the rest, as they say, is history.

A privileged generation

Let's talk about Jesus' refusal to display signs and wonders around the time of his death. Does this mean that Jesus wanted people to believe he is God without seeing any proof? Of course Jesus wanted people to see proof, but he wouldn't be manipulated. Jesus understands the problem of our wanting to see with our own eyes. 'How privileged you all are to see the wonderful miracles my Father has done,' he once said to his disciples who saw again and again how Jesus manifested the power of God through signs and wonders. 'Many an ancient prophet and godly man and woman longed to see these days, and to see and hear what you have seen and heard!' (Luke 10:23-24). He wasn't kidding about being privileged. Most Christians living since the days of the apostles have been locked into a comparatively dreary, unglamorous church life with little or no dramatic evidence to validate their faith in Christ. Gone are the burning bushes, pillars of fire, voices from heaven. Gone for the most part are the healings, the mass conversions, and the exorcisms – the casting out of demons. Perhaps worst of all, gone, too, are the opportunities to sit at Jesus' feet in the flesh to hear him explain the riddles of the ages in simple, often humorous terms, before moving on to describe our glorious destiny with him.

At the start of this chapter, I described how people say that if God would only show them a miracle, they would believe in him. Many look first for evidence that God's power is real, but even seeing it, they often don't recognise it.

Ironically, seeing does not make one believe. Jesus knew this and he said to his apostles:

> You are permitted to know some truths about the kingdom
> of God that are hidden to those outside the kingdom:

'Though they see and hear, they will not understand or turn to God, or be forgiven for their sins' (Mark 4:11-12, *Living Bible*).

Believing is seeing

When I was at university, I had a favourite English professor whom I'll call Dr Jones. One day we were discussing some poetry, which prompted Dr Jones to refer to the above passage. According to my teacher, this proved that Christianity is hopelessly elitist, a club that only accepts the initiated.

I had only recently been converted to Christianity after years of being an agnostic. Other than the fact that I knew I had given my life to Jesus, my knowledge of Christian doctrine could have been summed up on a small index card! (Some reading this book might say that's still the case. Though if you've bothered to read this far, maybe I'm making some sense!)

Nevertheless, green as I was, I knew Dr Jones was wrong. A washed-out Cub Scout and an angry rebel from the Church from about age 11, I was far from an initiate of some ecclesiastical clique.

My first halting step towards embracing Christianity occurred one night when I was about age 17. I was staggering down a city street with some friends after a party. We happened across a nondescript man standing under a lamppost preaching the gospel. This was too much fun to pass up, so we stopped and listened. Then I began to fire questions at him: 'Wasn't Jesus really an astronaut?' 'Wasn't the Bible rewritten by some medieval popes?' 'What happens to babies that die without being baptised?' 'Isn't Jesus just a myth like Santa Claus?' Hardly allowing him to reply to one question, I asked still more questions until we got tired of that sport. I simply laughed and walked away when he warned us that sinners needed to repent and accept Jesus as our 'personal saviour' before it was too late.

I'm sure that night this poor man trudged home discouraged, telling his wife that he was a miserable failure. Yet, oddly enough, what I had heard him say made sense to me. Whether it was my early Catholic training, or an act of the Holy Spirit, I don't know; however, even as an agnostic, I was aware of sin in my own life (though I doubt at the time that I would have called it that) and I wanted to change. This street preacher said that only Jesus could change me. That offer appealed to me. So as a result of that lively twenty-minute encounter under a street lamp, I decided to make my own investigations into the claims of the Bible – a book I had never opened, let alone studied. The result of my study was I became convinced that Jesus was an historical figure and that he had said and done some pretty remarkable things. Soon, however, my interest in Jesus waned and life went on pretty much as usual.

A few months later, my older brother Frank came home from university and announced that he had 'accepted Jesus as his saviour'. He gave me a book that convinced me that whether you were a Catholic, a Protestant, a Jew, a Hindu or a Muslim, Jesus was the road to God. As Peter said of Jesus to the Sanhedrin, 'And there is salvation in no one else, for there is no other name under heaven given among men by which we must be saved' (Acts 4:12).

At the end of the book, the author asked if I would like to have 'a relationship with Jesus'. I was astonished to see that to begin a relationship with God, all people had to do was repent of their sins and ask Jesus to come into their lives (Acts 10:43). I closed the book, set it aside, and knelt on the floor of my mother's living room and prayed the sinner's prayer: *Lord Jesus, I am sorry for the bad things I have done. I ask you to forgive me, and I now turn away from everything I know to be wrong. Thank you for dying on the cross to set me free from my sins. Please come into my life and fill me with your Holy Spirit and be my personal saviour. Thank you, Lord Jesus, Amen.* It was that simple!

Up until then, I think that I was expecting some great sign to be presented to me like Constantine's fiery cross in the sky before I would believe. 'Show me!' had been my motto. Nothing like this happened. I simply became convinced that Jesus is the Son of God and he died for my sins, and that he would raise me from the dead one day to live with him, as it says in the Apostles' Creed.

As a youngster, I had often repeated this creed in churches, but it didn't make any sense to me. Yet, in a calm, rational moment, I simply believed. There were no supernatural manifestations. No special sensation. Nothing but a profound assurance of my salvation. This is how most people come to faith, with some dramatic exceptions.

Jesus still mostly ignores demands for miracles as a means of converting the unbeliever. After all, the apostles watched Jesus closely for three years. They saw his wonderful miracles. Yet all promptly forgot them and scattered when Christ was arrested – despite what they had seen with their own eyes. Would we be any different?

In some inexplicable way, it is actually better to believe without seeing. Note the irony in Jesus' words: 'You believe because you have seen me. But blessed are those who haven't seen me [and my signs and wonders] and believe anyway' (John 20:29, *Living Bible*).

Certainly, we must look foolish in the eyes of non-believers when we give away 10 per cent of our income, forgive our enemies, and love the unlovely – all for the love of an unseen God. As St Augustine wrote: *Faith must hold what it cannot behold.*

Although the existence of God may not be proved in a laboratory or a courtroom, evidence of it may be found everywhere, usually during some moral, political, or personal failure. In the next chapter, we'll look at some examples of what I mean.

---

1. For an excellent narrative treatment of this, see C. S. Lewis' *The Lion, the Witch and the Wardrobe*, in which the Lion, Aslan, a Christ symbol, gives his life to save Edmund Pevensie. While this story offers rich insight to the crucifixion, death and resurrection of Jesus, it in no way parallels the gospel accounts. Nevertheless, this story helps people to understand why Jesus had to die, shedding light on the doctrines of atonement, rebirth, and resurrection.

CHAPTER THIRTEEN

How to fail successfully

If you want to know how to fail successfully, study the life of John Wesley, a truly successful failure. Wesley was an eighteenth-century theologian, evangelist, and the founder of Methodism. Born to the Rev Samuel and Susannah Wesley in 1703, he was educated at Charterhouse School and Christ Church, Oxford. After distinguishing himself as a scholar, he took Holy Orders and later became a fellow at Lincoln College, Oxford.

While at Lincoln, he and younger brother Charles formed the Holy Club that included evangelist George Whitefield. The club members practised a strict and therefore methodical form of Christianity that focused on good works such as visiting prisons and hospitals and giving alms to the poor. A brilliant mind, an enviable academic career, approval and admiration from devoted followers: in every way, life couldn't have been better for Wesley. Although some of his contemporaries ignored Wesley, branding him a 'methodist' because of his rigid doctrines, for all intents and purposes, he was a success.

But John Wesley was not satisfied. In his heart, he felt that there was more he could do for God. The mid-eighteenth century saw the birth of the modern missionary movement. The most likely place to go for an enterprising would-be missionary like John Wesley was the New World – specifically, the American Colonies. Typically, Wesley set his sights on the roughest of the colonies – the penal colony of Georgia – which, unknown to him at the time, was to be his Waterloo.

After much preparation and intense prayer, Wesley sailed to Georgia in 1735 as an Anglican missionary. He wanted to see his brand of Anglicanism imprinted on that budding civilisation, but his real prize would be to convert the native Americans.

On the voyage across the Atlantic, he befriended Moravian Christians, whose evangelical devoutness greatly impressed him. Halfway across the ocean a violent storm blew up, and at one stage it was thought the ship was about to sink. In the midst of the squall, the Moravians calmly held a prayer meeting in which they praised God while the rest of the crew and passengers panicked, including John Wesley. Wesley was amazed to see that this group of foreign Christians were not afraid to die. The fact that the Moravians had peace but Wesley had none piqued him. *Why? Was there more to the Christian faith than merely doing good deeds?*

Apparently there was. Count Nikolaus Ludwig Graf von Zinzendorf was a German religious reformer who led the Renewed Church of the Unity of the Brethren (Moravians). Count Von Zinzendorf told Wesley that being an Anglican, a Baptist, a Presbyterian, a Catholic, a Moravian – or indeed, being a member of any denomination – does *not* make you a Christian. Unless you are 'born again' you are not a part of God's family. Full stop. This is the meaning of John 3:3: 'Jesus replied, "I assure you, unless you are born again, you can never see the Kingdom of God"' (NLT). This point is repeated again in John 3:7: 'So don't be surprised at my statement that you must be born again' (NLT).

When the weather improved, Wesley came to no firm conclusions one way or the other about his need to be born again. Moreover, after land was sighted, the would-be evangelist shrugged off Von Zinzendorf's words as so much piety and prepared to take the colony of Georgia and the native Americans for Christ and his Kingdom.

Many excellent biographers have documented Wesley's short stay in Georgia. Suffice to say that his legalistic brand of Christianity, as well as his aloof behaviour, offended all strata of Georgian society. All ignored him, from the transported convicts, to the German Jews, the Scots, and the Irish, right up to the British philanthropist James Oglethorpe, the Governor of the Colony. Wesley had little if any dealings with the natives, which is probably a good thing, as no doubt they also would have rejected his attempts at converting them to his brand of Christianity, and maybe even made him a martyr for his trouble. Quite simply, Wesley's American experience was a flop.

In 1988 I made a four-part documentary on the life of John Wesley for BBC Radio Oxford, entitled 'John Wesley – Man of God'. While researching it, I was surprised to learn that had Wesley not fled the colony and escaped back to England in 1738, he would have been arrested by Oglethorpe, tried as a criminal, and flung in jail. One biographer told me that the reason why Governor Oglethorpe wanted Wesley arrested is that Wesley had allegedly proposed marriage to his niece but then defaulted. Wesley claims he never proposed, but that the impressionable young woman had misconstrued his intentions. In any case, this was a punishable offence, and Wesley fled Georgia by cover of night.

This was not how John Wesley had expected his mission to turn out. Up until then, he had succeeded in turning every circumstance to his own advantage. All of a sudden, he was a fugitive, a failed missionary, a debtor, a promise-breaker, and in the eyes of his family and friends, a quitter. On the trip home, he feared he would lose his faith altogether. Then he recalled the need to be born again.

In London, Wesley again sought out the Moravians; while attending one of their meetings in Aldersgate Street, London, on 24 May 1738, he experienced a spiritual rebirth that profoundly convinced him that salvation was gained not through good deeds, but by placing faith in Jesus Christ alone. That night he recorded in his journal that his heart had been 'strangely warmed'. Thereafter, his attempts at preaching the Gospel produced the kind of results that he had failed to see in Georgia.

John Wesley's influence was felt around the world, but as is often the case, a prophet is rarely appreciated at home. British bishops and clergy frowned on Wesley's 'enthusiasm' and disliked his penchant for 'revivalism', and so one by one, the pulpits were closed to him. The most famous censure was the edict made by the Bishop of Oxford. He proclaimed that Wesley may no longer preach in the pulpits of the city of dreaming spires – the same city where some two hundred years before Wesley, Thomas Cranmer was burned at the stake for his 'enthusiasm', and approximately 200 years after Wesley, C. S. Lewis was humiliated for writing books about the Christian faith that could be understood by the masses. (So *what* is Oxford's problem?)

In a classic case of a man not leaving his church, rather his church leaving him, Wesley had no choice but to preach outdoors or in private rooms thereafter. Despite initial misgivings about preaching in the open, Wesley became convinced that open-air preaching was the most effective way to reach the masses.

A man who seemed to need little or no sleep, Wesley covered over 5000 miles a year on horseback, and his private journals show that he frequently preached five sermons a day! His tracts and books were mass-produced cheaply so that even the poorest could afford to purchase and read his sermons. Think of the effect that he would have had if radio and television had been invented in his day![1]

A man of many parts, Wesley went beyond biblical exegesis. A scientific man, he taught about the need for public health and sanitation. Indeed, he is the author of *Primitive Physic*, an early medical text which, quaint by today's standards, was in its day highly acclaimed. He also penned the *General Receipt Book*, a book of scientific recipes that included a section on making wine! He also advocated learning to read and the need for widespread education, a tenet of Methodism continued to this day. A social reformer, his revival sermons not only fought sin and ignorance but they also went some way to elevate the status of Jews, Catholics, women and other oppressed groups. Consequently, whether or not they agree with his religious convictions, most historians say Wesley's preaching saved Britain from the ravages of an insurrection similar to the French Revolution (1789 to 1799).

His influence went well beyond the British Isles. Wesley opposed slavery when it was still a legal and lucrative business. Hence, he is indirectly credited with ending the British slave trade (1807) and the European slave trade (1814). Later, with the help of Methodists and other Christian groups, the American slave trade came under attack and officially ended in 1863 under President Abraham Lincoln, who was not afraid to employ biblical principles when it came to making public policy.[2]

Later, the Methodists influenced the creation of unions, implemented humane labour laws, reformed child labour practices and proposed a host of other enlightened social legislation which today we take for granted.

Arguably, John Wesley's Georgian failure was the start of the making of the great man he was eventually to become. But the Georgia debacle was not to be the last, or even the greatest, of his failures. In 1751, at the age of 48, Wesley married Mary Vazeille, a widow with four children. The marriage was an unhappy and an unfulfilled union, producing no children of their own. Eventually, Mary Vazeille-Wesley deserted John, a stigma which in some denominations would have meant Wesley would have had to resign from the ministry.

The lesson of John Wesley and other successful failures

As we near the end of this book on failure, we have seen how many men and women have learned from their mistakes, mistakes that had the potential to destroy their faith, their credibility and, ultimately, their contributions to society.

Someone once said that in order to be a good teacher, it helps to be a good failure. Although this is a platitude, there is at least a grain of truth in it. After all, we can learn a great deal from a person who has attempted many things, and failed, even if all we learn is to avoid that person's mistakes.

But failure is not just about learning from past mistakes. Failure is proactive, too. Successful failures don't allow the past to destroy them; they use their failures to improve their future strategy.

Billy Graham talks about his colossal failure in judgement made in the 1960s by allowing himself to become aligned with the Republican political party in general and President Nixon in particular. In the aftermath of the scandal of

Watergate, Nixon's political future was dead, and many of Graham's critics predicted that the evangelist's credibility was extinct too. But Graham publicly repented of his mistakes, privately confessed his sins, and completely trusted God to show him the way forward.

Billy Graham knew that with God all things are possible (note this doesn't imply, therefore, that with God all things are easy!), and so he humbly carried on in the teeth of withering criticism throughout the 70s and 80s, hoping for the best. Today, older and wiser, he no longer mixes faith with party politics. The result is his credibility is higher than ever. I recommend Graham's approach any time we fail – be it at business, in our marriage, or in any of scores of possible endeavours. Above all, remember that Christianity is about new beginnings, not past hurts.

The apostle Paul, no stranger to personal failure, says we are saved by hope (Romans 8:24). The late Jack Clemo was a writer who became addicted to hope. Jack lost his father at an early age, leaving his mother to bring him up as best she could. Although he was a healthy baby, he lost his eyesight as a boy, the result of an incurable illness. Despite his handicap, he determined to earn his living as a writer.[3]

Over the years, Jack received one rejection slip after another, but he still wrote – short stories, poems, and even letters to the editors of local newspapers. At last, he found success when his novel *Wilding Graft* was published, winning for him an Atlantic Award.

In his mid-thirties, Clemo became totally deaf. Because novelists depend on creating credible characters, they need to be able to mimic the nuances, the accents, and the current slang to make dialogue come alive. In this sense, novelists need their ears more than they need their eyes! Consequently,

Jack's deafness ended his career as a novelist just as he was beginning to succeed. Gradually, he turned to other forms of expressing himself, including writing essays and autobiographies. But the rejection slips continued to fall through his mail slot like dead autumn leaves. Soon he and his mother were living in abject poverty, his writing netting only a few pounds now and then.

Despite the extreme frustration, towards the end of his life, Jack said his failure was a blessing – to himself and others. Although he was bitter for many years, his disappointment drove him to embrace a deeper Christian faith, a faith that prompted him to write poetry, the language of the inner eye and ear. Jack told me in a letter dated 22 August 1983 that he was aware that his 'literary struggles and setbacks [have] encouraged young Christian writers who are also getting their work rejected by brisk commercial publishers, the secular market, or rigidly conventional Christian firms.'

I can attest to this last point. When I first started out as a journalist, I couldn't find a full-time job, and my book and article proposals had drawn mainly rejection slips from publishers. Each failure felt like the stinging lash of a whip on my back.

Early in 1984 I wrote in my journal, 'My future is in the hands of strange men and women – personnel directors, secretaries, editors, publishers – and I am utterly and completely lacking the adequate tools to fend for myself. If I am feeling sorry for myself (and I do) I feel sorrier for my wife. She has married a useless idealist.' But Jack's friendly letters inspired me to continue when there was little or no hope for my writing career.

An unexpected letter from Jack written on 10 April 1984 made my spirits soar. Among other things Jack wrote:

'I do hope and pray you will succeed somewhere – Christian writers must make an impact, or the pagan humanist set will have a monopoly . . . We hope to have some batches of good news from you in the next few years.' Encouragement from a man whose own struggles were so great was like getting a letter from Jesus himself assuring me that 'All will be well. Don't give up. I am with you!' Perhaps there is someone you will be able to encourage as the result of having lived through your own personal hell and finding that God is indeed faithful. In that sense, all failure is potentially helpful to us and to others we know.

Failure is relative

In 1993, I flew with Baroness Caroline Cox to Armenia and Russia to make a film about a low intensity but deadly war going on between impoverished Armenia and oil-rich Azerbaijan over the disputed territory of Nagorno-Karabakh. The frightful conditions under which these Christian Armenians live and die taught me that most of my failures are trivial in comparison to what is going on there. I'm glad I went because I learned that God offers us hope in every kind of circumstance – even when Christians are being ethnically cleansed by Islamic militants for political reasons. For a fuller treatment of this and related issues, see *Baroness Cox – A Voice for the Voiceless* (Lion, 1998), by Andrew Boyd, a man whom I consider to be one of Britain's most talented Christian journalists.

Here are some vignettes from other places around the world to show that human failure never stops God's purposes.

A light in the darkness

In 1966, Mao Tse-Tung led a Communist-inspired coup in China known as the Cultural Revolution, an outrageous example of political and social failure. Under Mao, Christianity was outlawed and hundreds of ministers lost their licence to preach, countless hundreds were martyred, and thousands of Christians lost their livelihood. This upheaval lasted until Mao's death in 1976. Beginning in 1977, China abandoned the Cultural Revolution's radical socio-economic policies. Today, Chinese Christians may worship openly. Bibles are freely distributed. Even a few government officials profess faith in Jesus Christ. Whereas a mere 35 years ago there were roughly one million Christians, now accurate estimates are impossible to establish due to rapid church growth across all denominations in China.

What has caused this massive increase in believers? No one knows for sure. One thing is certain, however, millions of new disciples were made during the darkest period in Chinese Church history when the Church may be said to have failed as an institution. God seems to work best when, humanly speaking, all seems lost. Ironically, times of failure – not good times – may be a key to understanding church growth.

When all was lost, God came in

Chen (not her real name) discovered the power of hope not long ago. Chen is a Chinese Christian who was tortured and imprisoned for her faith by the Communists. 'We hate Christians,' she was told over and over by a prison official. After a particularly brutal beating administered by two prison guards, she was flung into a cell with two hardened female criminals who ignored her bloody cuts and bruises. It was clear to Chen that her cellmates hated her, too. With no first aid, and the very real possibility of all three women receiving the death penalty, Chen lay on the floor praying silently.

All night long Chen heard her cellmates wail and groan – although the two women were brutal, they both feared dying. When Chen was strong enough to move about, she was filled with compassion for her cellmates. The Holy Spirit told her to be kind to them in practical ways.

Chen decided to fast, giving her meagre portion of food to the perplexed women who gobbled it down in case she changed her mind. Never having received kindness in their lives, the pair were deeply touched by Chen.

Gradually Chen realised why she had been put in prison – to tell these two women about God. Chen told them about Jesus, explaining that he was the Lord of lords. This made sense to the women, as they had been under the power of one lord or another all their lives. Chen pointed out that although Jesus was their Lord, he loved them and wanted to bless them. Feeling hopeful about life for the first time since childhood, the two women asked how they could know Jesus as their personal Lord and saviour, too.

The women knelt and made an open profession to Christ in their cell. As believers they would receive worse treatment – even death – but suddenly they no longer dreaded dying. After this, these women preached hope in the depths of that depressing prison. Everyone was affected by their serenity, especially the prison governor.

The cheerful behaviour of a Christian prisoner thrown into a living nightmare eventually led to an early release for all three women who continued to preach to anyone who would listen to them.

Britain's Christian heritage

Our nation is in a stage of moral decay. Secularism is on the rise. Pessimism reigns in our schools, our political institutions, the media, and in society at large. One well-known commentator has said that Britain has reinvented failure as a lifestyle, and a well-known Catholic bishop has said Christianity has failed in Britain. But with God's help, even one person can change our nation. Remember, 'All authority in heaven and on earth has been given to us in Jesus' name' (Matthew 28:18, RSV). Nothing robs us of hope (and therefore authority) like failure. But it needn't.

Notice how the following British Christians affected the nation for good despite personal failures:

- Plagued with debt and a disappointing political career, Lord Shaftesbury championed the cause of the poor and brought about the beginning of social welfare for Britain's neediest people.

- Craving a husband's love and a home of her own, and being in poor health, Florence Nightingale nevertheless birthed the modern nursing movement, invented battlefield hygiene, and injected Christian ethics into the field of medicine.

- Although his British film company lost him great deal of money before he sold it in the 1960s, J. Arthur Rank is credited with having beaten the Hollywood movie moguls Samuel Goldwin, Otto Preminger and Jack Warner at their own game in the 1940s, the heyday of studio movie making. His formula for success? 'I try to make films that honour God.'

As Paul wrote, 'For the sake of Christ, then, I am content with weaknesses, insults, hardships, persecutions, and calamities; for when I am weak, then I am strong' (2 Corinthians 12:10).

1. Of course, Wesley would not be permitted to preach on the air if he lived today thanks to the current laws that govern what Christians may do or say on British airwaves. For a fuller discussion of this matter use an Internet search engine and key in *Christian Broadcasting UK* and look for topics about the 1990 Broadcasting Act, UCB, or Ban on Christian Broadcasters. Or write to The Christian Institute, 26 Jesmond Road, Newcastle upon Tyne, NE2 4PQ; telephone 0191 281 566; e-mail: info@christian.org.uk; website: www.christian.org.uk. It will open your eyes to a terrible injustice.

2. The Methodists joined with American Abolitionists, which led to the Emancipation Proclamation (1 January 1863) and the end of American slavery under Abraham Lincoln, a committed Christian, who declared all slaves in the United States forever free.

3. Jack's full story is recounted in his two autobiographies, *Confession of a Rebel* (Chatto and Windus, 1975) and *The Marriage of a Rebel* (Gollancz, 1980); his poetry appears in a variety of anthologies.

CHAPTER FOURTEEN

The light of failure

There was an accident in a Welsh coal mine. An entire section of an underground passage had collapsed, trapping ten men. Nine miners were cut off from the main shaft. One man had escaped being sealed off with the others because he was nearest the entrance of the collapsed passageway. Nonetheless, he was pinned from the waist down beneath a pile of shattered timber and stone.

Immediately, a rescue team was dispatched with lanterns, picks and shovels. When they came across this man, they began to dig him out. He adamantly waved them away, shouting, 'No, no. Leave me. I'll be all right.' Jabbing his thumb in the direction of the blocked mine shaft, he warned, 'The lads'll suffocate behind that pile unless you start digging them out now! Just leave me some tools and go on ahead. I'll dig myself out!' Seeing that the man was in no pain, they gave him a lamp and a shovel and moved further down the tunnel.

Using the shovel as a lever and a rock as a fulcrum, the miner moved several large stones and some splintered beams off his legs. When at last, he removed most of the debris, he picked up the lantern and took a look at his lower half. Suddenly, his eyes widened and he began to wail pitifully for the others to come back and help him. His right leg had been severed above the knee by a sharp piece of metal. He knew that only emergency medical attention would prevent his bleeding to death!

When it comes to God's offer of salvation, many of us are like that self-sufficient coal miner. We feel that God's offer is not an urgent need in our lives, although we may know of many others who surely need God's help. So we wave God on and give our attention to the day-to-day routine of working, paying bills, playing, and sleeping when in fact we are in great jeopardy spiritually.

The miner was blissfully ignorant of his life's blood draining out of his body into the gritty soil of the mine shaft until he held up his light and saw himself as he really was. Mercifully, his story had a happy ending – although the man lost his leg, he saved his life.

Sometimes failure can be the light that shows people their true condition. When everything is going smoothly, we tend to think that we don't need God's help, thank you very much. It's easy enough to fall prey to this sort of thinking, too. But through failure, we see clearly how weak and helpless we actually are. Failure proves to us that we are not self-sufficient. This is another reason why God allows Christians to fail.

Humiliation, sexual frustration, and a broken heart – the story of Dorothy L. Sayers

Dorothy L. Sayers, celebrated detective novelist and respected scholar, suffered a broken love affair that was followed by a profound social failure. Later on, she was married to a man who was difficult to love. Put simply, despite her fame as a writer, Sayers knew what it meant to be a failure.

As did so many of her generation, Sayers grew up accepting the teaching of the Church of England. By the time she had left Oxford University, she probably suspected that for most people, the Christian faith was a comfortable habit – the backdrop to a conventional life. On one hand, she was used to churchgoing and regular liturgical worship, but on the other, she was acutely aware that there was no heart in much of what passed as Christianity: it seemed bloodless, mundane, and cold. Out of sheer convention, she continued to go to church.

In early adulthood, Dorothy Sayers fell in love with an artistically refined, but emotionally crude man who was incapable of returning Sayers' intense affection. While publishing brought in enough money to live, Sayers was lonely and unfulfilled romantically for years. To compensate, she sought amorous fulfilment in the Bohemian set of Soho and Bloomsbury. But this, too, proved unsatisfactory.

Soon the novelist dropped all artistic airs as well as her Christian prudence. She sought instead fun and free sex with a plain, uneducated man who enjoyed boating, drinking, smoking and dancing. Her highbrow friends and colleagues wondered what she saw in this man: they could hardly imagine what the couple talked about – she a brilliant Oxford graduate, and he an uncouth mechanic. But he gave her a good time – as well as a son. Of course, Sayers wanted to marry her lover, but she had managed once again to land herself with a cold and belligerent man. He did not have the slightest interest in Sayers, or their child, who was eventually sent to live in Oxford with a relative. Sayers succumbed to the failure she had hoped to escape, only now she had to accept the added responsibility of supporting a fatherless son.

No longer holding out for romance or a proper church wedding, Sayers eventually met and married a divorced journalist some years her senior. They were not in love in the conventional sense of the word.

Sayers is too complex a character to be treated in so cursory a manner, but suffice to say that it was because her life had plumbed the depths that she was able to discover that what she really needed more than anything else was the light – a living relationship with God through Jesus Christ.

Sayers' new-found faith showed through in almost everything she wrote from that time on, particularly *The Man Born to be King*, a retelling of the life of Christ using modern speech. She was criticised for creating a plain-speaking Christ, but, she explained, she wanted ordinary people to understand Jesus' words. Up until then, Jesus was always represented in stilted, two-dimensional terms, speaking in an otherworldly King James English.

Over two million people heard *The Man Born to be King* when it was first broadcast on the BBC, and for many in Britain, it was the first time they ever thought of Jesus as being human. It's said that many people found faith following those broadcasts, which pleased Sayers.

Failure became her mentor. If Sayers had not faced humiliation, sexual frustration, and – to some extent – the threat of financial failure, Christianity might have remained for her no more than a watered-down, man-made religion. No doubt Dorothy Sayers would have eventually turned her keen intellect against the Church in the manner of George Bernard Shaw, Bertrand Russell, and Albert Camus and scores of others whose iconoclastic messages have influenced modern thought to such a great extent. James Brabazon, Sayers' biographer, claims that her evangelical zeal was not so much the result of her own salvation, but more as a result of her understanding of the sordidness of sin.

Fear God, not failure

Don't be afraid of failure. Keep on going in spite of it. 'The fear of the Lord is the beginning of knowledge; fools despise wisdom and instruction' (Proverbs 1:7). The word *fear* is translated *respect*. Out of respect, we should worship God until success comes. The hardest part of faith is suffering. But if you keep on going forward, you will surely overcome the obstacle. Paul writes: 'No temptation [problem] has overtaken you that is not common to man. God is faithful, and he will not let you be tempted beyond your strength, but with the temptation will also provide the way of escape, that you may be able to endure it' (1 Corinthians 10:13). This doesn't mean, of course, that things will work out exactly the way we planned them. It does mean, however, that God will make a way forward that will meet our every need as our friends Bob and Marge discovered.

Career failure and cancer – Bob and Marge's story

My wife and I met Bob and Marge (not their real names) while we lived in Oxford. Bob had brought his family of five to England from the United States in order to work on a DPhil in theology. As the years passed, Bob set his heart on becoming a university professor. He felt ill-suited to preaching and pastoral work. My wife and I knew that Bob and Marge had sacrificed much – both financially and emotionally – in order for Bob to study at Oxford, but we had no doubts when they left for the United States that Bob would soon make his way in academia.

One Christmas we received a letter from Marge. She told us that one teaching post after another had been closed to Bob, but finally Bob accepted a job looking after a small church in the Midwest. At the same time, a routine check-up showed that Marge had breast cancer and had to have immediate surgery to remove her left breast.

To make a long story short, Bob became a minister and learned to like it. And Marge was grateful not to have to undergo chemotherapy. We were wonderfully amazed – in spite of all our *why* questions – that our friends could still rejoice with thankfulness and humility in this unwelcome series of events.

I don't like to think about the type of Christmas card I might have sent if I were in Bob and Marge's situation, yet I know that their attitude was the key to their peacefulness at that time. Nevertheless, I am learning from Bob and Marge of the need to keep faith in the midst of a great failure as King David, no stranger to failure, wrote:

> In times of trouble, may the Lord respond to your cry. May the God of Israel keep you safe from all harm. May he send you help from his sanctuary and strengthen you from Jerusalem (Psalms 20:1-2).

Staying the course

Only one in ten people who make a commitment to Christ are still following him ten years later. Why do some people hold on to their faith but not others? I don't know. But it happens.[1] Compare King David, who remained faithful, to King Saul, who lost his faith.

King David had the faith to come before the Lord despite being a murderer and adulterer, asking for the forgiveness he knew he would receive. King Saul, who merely disobeyed God, chose to fall on his sword instead of asking God to forgive him for his sin, a relatively minor infraction compared to David's heinous crimes (see 1 Samuel 31:1-5 and 2 Samuel 12:7-15). Why?

Consider the apostles Peter and Judas. Peter retained the faith to know that Christ would forgive him for denying him – not once but three times, while Judas condemned himself to death for one act of betrayal. Again, why?

There is no sure answer to these questions. However, I do know this: Saul and Judas fell for one of Satan's surest ploys – self-judgement.

Better off dead?

Both Saul and Judas set out to serve God. Both men achieved some success as well. Saul's early exploits against the enemies of Israel made him seem a wise and fearless leader. In many ways, he was. However, Saul liked to do things his way, and so he got into trouble by disobeying the Lord's mouthpiece, the prophet Samuel. Even when Saul was actively working against God's will, he could have repented and stepped down from his high position in humility and found full pardon. But instead, he led a disastrous campaign against the Philistines, and Israel was defeated.

Overcome by his failure and the news of the death of his own sons, and acutely aware of his failures, Saul begged his armour bearer to kill him. He would not. Again, Saul might have repented, accepting his defeat as punishment. Instead, he gave in to pride and despair. Judging himself unredeemable – a fatal and relatively rare condition for any human being (Mark 3:29) – Saul tumbled forward onto the razor-sharp point of his sword and snuffed out his life.

Betrayal, self-pity and suicide – Judas' story

Judas Iscariot had been a trusted member of Christ's inner circle of twelve and had the respectable task of looking after the money purse. Many people have depicted Judas in different ways. One popular view represents him as a man acting out of noble motives. Judas, believing that Jesus was the Messiah, betrayed Christ in order to prompt Christ to assume his rightful role as the political deliverer of all of Israel. He, therefore, acted in good faith in betraying his master because the end justified the means. Conversely, in all three synoptic Gospels, Judas is described as an outsider and a traitor. John frankly calls Judas a 'thief' and says he was 'possessed by the devil'. This would suggest that Judas acted either out of jealousy or out of criminal intent and greed.

Whatever motivated Judas to act, he eventually gave in to self-judgement. That Judas felt deep remorse for his actions is undeniable. Seeing his master meekly submit to the mob rather than defend himself, Judas charged back to the chief priests and cast the thirty pieces of silver at their feet, which they piously refused to receive. Deeply dejected, he turned and fled into the night (Matthew 27:3-4).

If ever there was a time when Satan confronted Judas, it must have been now. 'See what you've done, Judas?' the evil one might have whispered into the agitated man's ear. 'You've made a total wreck of your career as an apostle, and, what's more, you've ruined the lives of the other apostles who depended on you. And, worst of all, you scum, you've wasted the life of the good rabbi. No one will forgive you for this.' Satan would have laughed sarcastically, adding, 'You may as well go kill yourself. The world will be better off without you!' Within the hour, Judas was dead by his own hand (Matthew 27:5).

It is wrong to assume that we have totally failed in this life. Actually, we won't know the results until we die. Meantime, we must move forward bravely and know that there is a good purpose behind all that happens in our lives. As Paul writes: 'And I am sure that he who began a good work in you will bring it to completion at the day of Jesus Christ (Philippians 1:6).

Satan's lies always prompt rash action. Had Judas not given in to the urge to become his own judge and jury, an acute form of self-pity, he would have been wildly ecstatic in only three days when the empty tomb was discovered.

I've made a mess of my life

If you have failed at some important task, or if you feel you've made a complete mess of your life, and, as the result, you are thinking about suicide: *don't do it*. Wait. The main reason you want to end it all is to be rid of the bad feelings associated with your failure. Satan would dearly love you to act now, to take your life immediately rather than seek out other ways to resolve your problems.

When I have failed and felt discouraged, I have benefited from close contact with other believers whom I trust and respect. Talk is not cheap – and it is very therapeutic. Talking to someone else could have saved Saul and Judas. It could help you. Even if you are not a Christian, you can still find many sympathetic listeners. Christians aren't the only ones who care about people!

Remember, whether you are a Christian or not, God loves you and Satan hates you. No matter how terribly you have failed, God understands and wants to comfort you. God's love is enduring – just check out 1 Corinthians 13:4-7:

> Love is patient and kind; love is not jealous or boastful; it is not arrogant or rude. Love does not insist on its own way; it is not irritable or resentful; it does not rejoice at wrong, but rejoices in the right. Love bears all things, believes all things, hopes all things, endures all things.

Hate, which is the devil's stock in trade, is the total opposite of love: *hate is impatient, harsh, jealous, boastful, irritable, resentful, rejoices at wrong, tolerates nothing, doubts everything, is pessimistic, and endures nothing.* Satan wants you to feel a humiliated and unloved failure. He wants you to lose hope and commit suicide. He wants you to be like him. Remember, misery loves company.

This may be a wicked and sinful world, but love still remains and always will until the Lord returns for his people. So there is always a reason to go on living in the knowledge that, no matter how bleak and hopeless a situation may be, this, too, shall pass. As we saw in Judas' case, even postponing a planned suicide for a few days and talking it over with someone who can be objective can make all the difference in how you perceive yourself and your situation.

Suicide doesn't solve any problems. Most often it causes more. In every case I have known, the family and friends – the ones left behind – suffer as the result of the suicide, often leading to more depression, disharmony and even more suicide.

Moreover, what lies beyond death? At least while you live, you may find ways to overcome your problems. Once you have crossed the line into infinity, it's too late to go back. Many opt for suicide as a means of finding everlasting peace, either in a sweet sleep or in the comfort of unconscious oblivion. I doubt that death is like that. You may be taking your problems with you, and possibly finding that in death, there is no way to escape them.

My own experiences with failure have taught me one sure thing – nothing is irreparable. When I have plumbed the depths of despair – and that's been many times – I have resisted the temptation to indulge in self-pity. Now looking back on those times, I see that the pain that I felt has passed and the problems have either righted themselves or have been long forgotten.

What is certain?

Nowhere in the Bible is there a promise that any that have decided to follow God will be spared pain, suffering, and failure. In fact, often to be a Christian is more difficult than rejecting faith.

This is certain: each of us is destined to carry our cross – carry it, but not to die on it. Christ died on the cross once and for all, *halleluia*! (I couldn't resist that.) If we are to follow Christ, then we must accept a share of failure, grief, pain, anguish, shame, or despair while serving him on this side of paradise. We must turn from self to God and say, as did Jesus, 'Not my will but yours, Father.' Someone once said, 'A man is no fool to give up the things he can't keep in order to gain the things he can't lose.' In doing this, we stand to lose all, but, paradoxically, we also stand to gain all, though not necessarily in a material sense.

Death, the ultimate human failure – *not!*

We have a very dear friend who recently died, leaving growing children and a grieving husband. I was making toast in the kitchen when the telephone rang in the next room.

'I'll get it,' called my wife. A few minutes later, I heard the receiver being placed back in the cradle.

'That was Sue,' she said. 'Martha died early this morning.' To be perfectly honest, my first reaction was envy. 'Well, if heaven's anything like I think it is, we don't need to pity *Martha*,' I said with confident male aplomb. 'No more bills to pay. No more failing health. No sadness.'

My wife glared at me. 'Why would God allow this to happen to someone as young as Martha?'

Reaching for the coffee-pot, I retorted crisply, 'Try to focus on what she's doing right *now*.' I heaped the coffee into the filter. 'It'll be one big party from the moment Martha entered into the gates of heaven.' I noticed I was feeling pangs of envy again.

'She had growing children.'

'Life will go on. *They'll* cope.' Suddenly, I recalled my father's death. He left my mother widowed at age 22 with two small children. We coped. But years later, I still cry about it.

'How is James going to raise the children alone?' I looked at my wife's face and I could see that she was upset.

'Look, you're asking all the wrong questions. If you had any idea how great heaven is, you'd be pleased that Martha's there now. James would, too.' Even I was struck by the hollowness of this comment. I finished my coffee and walked out of the kitchen.

Later that morning, I was feeling pretty angry about Martha's death. Oh, sure, I know the dead in Christ are with the Lord. But what about the people left behind to rebuild their broken lives alone?

C. S. Lewis faced that problem in *A Grief Observed*. In that book, Lewis recalls when his American wife, Joy Davidman-Gresham, was diagnosed with terminal cancer. First, they sought prayer for her cure, and thereafter, they believed for her healing. There came a brief remission, then the cancer returned, and Joy died a slow and agonising death.

Following her death, the man dubbed 'The Apostle to the Sceptics' found himself doubting everything he'd ever believed about God. The apologist who had written with certainty – some would say smugness – of God's goodness in *Mere Christianity* admits in *A Grief Observed* that the iron gates of heaven seemed to slam in his face during his intense distress. Lewis hadn't expected this reaction to her death. It's pretty powerful stuff.

The Hollywood version of Lewis' life, *Shadowlands*, leaves the viewer with the impression that Joy's death caused Lewis to lose his faith. He didn't. By the last pages of *A Grief Observed* we see that even though his heart had been lacerated by Joy's death, C. S. Lewis' faith in God remained intact.[2]

Death, like taxes, is a certainty, yet when it comes, few are prepared for it. The Church doesn't teach much about death and the afterlife these days. Malcolm Muggeridge said that 'death has become the dirty little secret that sex once was'. As a result, when death strikes, we have nothing to offer grieving people but platitudes and heretical distortions. What will the next life *really* be like?

In his sermon, 'The Weight of Glory', C. S. Lewis said if we could but foresee what each Christian is destined to become in the resurrection, we would fall down and worship them because they will be as glorious as Christ himself.

The image of the afterlife as some permanent Elysian Fields where disembodied souls dwell is a Pagan belief disguised as Christian doctrine. Eternal life is not about the immortality of the *soul*. Rather, it's about the immortality of the resurrected body. David Pawson points out that the Bible describes the new earth as a place where men and women will peacefully work and eat in immortal resurrected bodies.

The biblical fact of the resurrection needs to be understood by all believers. It should inform the whole Christian experience – our witnessing, our living, and, yes, our failing, our dying and our grieving.

So what about my friend Martha? Our reaction to the news of her death – envy, sadness, confusion, pain – was not altogether wrong. After all, Jesus wept when he learned of the death of his friend, Lazurus. Grief is about separation of family and friends. The pain is real and cannot be avoided. It is part of what it means to be human.

Christians must face the realities of this life honestly, knowing that they will have both good and bad experiences. It is our joy to thank God in the good times and our role to trust God in the bad. But if it were not for Christ's resurrection, we would be fools to adopt this way of thinking. As Paul writes to the Church in Corinth:

> For if the dead are not raised, then Christ has not been raised. If Christ has not been raised, your faith is futile and you are still in your sins. Then those also who have fallen asleep in Christ have perished. If for this life only we have hoped in Christ, we are of all men most to be pitied (1 Corinthians 15:16-19).

We must act upon this conviction. And then we will know that in spite of all outward appearances of failure, even in the face of our own death or the death of those we love, we must pick up our cross and carry it in our Lord's footsteps. Then we are living out our faith, a faith that requires willingness on our part to accept that God is always working on our behalf though all manner of circumstances. Again Paul reminds us:

> Not that I complain of want; for I have learned, in whatever state I am, to be content. I know how to be abased, and I know how to abound; in any and all circumstances I have learned the secret of facing plenty and hunger, abundance

and want. I can do all things in him who strengthens me (Philippians 4:11-13).

Paul's words are far from a stoic acceptance of all that happens, as if it is our fate. This attitude will only lead to bitterness and unhealthy anger towards God. Paul's final comment is the key to understanding how to find joy even in our failures. God doesn't say in Psalm 46:10: 'be numb and know that I am God'; rather he says, although all around you are agitated, you may 'be still'; when your best efforts seem to end in ignoble flames of defeat, 'rest assured'; when everybody else has abandoned you, 'Lo, I am with you always' (Matthew 28:20). These are not cheap words.

1. For a fuller discussion of this question, see *Once Saved, Always Saved* by David Pawson (Hodder & Stoughton, 1996).

2. Furthermore, Lewis' final book, *Letters to Malcolm: Chiefly on Prayer*, published posthumously (Geoffrey Bles, London, 1964), proves beyond a shadow of a doubt that Lewis died a firmly committed Christian and a pugnacious apologist for the faith.

Get involved in people's lives

There is a fine line between despairing and finding satisfaction, even joy, when we fail. If you have failed in some way, or if you know someone who has, the following seven suggestions are intended to turn your eyes off yourself and fix them on others. By practising these suggestions, you may become God's agent in helping to bring those who have failed back from the brink of despair.

1. God has no hands on earth but our hands

During the lowest ebbs in my own life, I have seen Christ most clearly through the loving action of others. Although it is tempting to turn our backs on another's failures, we *must* make ourselves available. It doesn't take a special talent to invite someone who is going through a hard time into your home for a meal. By creating a supportive environment and by *listening*, you may actually help others to recover self-esteem, confidence, and faith. Many times I hear people say they wish they knew what is God's will for their life. We all may be sure that part of the Lord's will is that we reach out and comfort the people who need our compassion and care (Romans 12:13; 1 Peter 4:9).

When my wife and I returned to England in 1985, we were expecting our first child. So we joined a church and settled down to the business of finding a place in the Oxford community. Although I knew finding media work in the United Kingdom would be tough, I had no idea of what I was about to go through. I was unemployed for almost a year and ineligible for the dole. As well as losing much of my confidence as a communicator, I began to feel paranoid, as if my being an American was keeping me from getting some of the jobs for which I had applied.

Judith and I had to spend most of our resources on daily living expenses. Soon our meagre savings had dwindled to nothing. Yet, each time we were down to our last few pennies, an envelope with money dropped though our mail slot, or we were invited out to a meal. Just occasionally, a friendly editor would ask me to do some writing.

At the time, our minister was the rector of St Aldates, Michael Green. I recall him giving us a big frozen chicken when he came to see us one time. These were surely miracles to us, but the miracles were carried out by members of our church family and friends – the Gunrajs, the Hills, the Fulfords, the Thomases, the Bruders; and individuals such as Sandy Cane, The Rev Bruce Gillingham, and Frank Entwhistle. There are, of course, many others too numerous to name but who know who they are. The small acts of kindness on the part of these people are what gave me the strength to keep on going after setbacks, defeats, failures and mistakes.

Everyone may become part of a miracle, if only they have a willingness to become part of another person's life, no matter how messy or complicated. This involvement is not only our Christian duty, it is also the way Christ works in us.

2. Don't wait for a crisis

I have a dear friend who once told me that as a Baptist

minister, he often meets people only after there is a problem. Having no prior relationship with them, it is hard to come alongside them and meet their needs. My friend makes a good point. It is impossible to offer much more than surface commiseration unless you are in a good relationship with as many people as possible.

My wife Judith is a good one for meeting newcomers to our church and inviting them home to meet our family. Over the years, she has had the opportunity to act as a sounding board for many women facing marriage problems, career setbacks, and any number of other heartbreaking failures. 'You'll meet people with needs everywhere,' she says. 'The question is, are you willing to get involved?' If you are, then, should a crisis arise, you'll be far better prepared to offer the right sort of assistance when it is needed. Remember, when Christ departed the earth 40 days after his resurrection, he didn't say to the disciples, 'Just call me if you need me'; instead he said, 'I am with you always, even to the end of the world' (Matthew 28:20). We must follow his example.

3. Become a prayer partner

A Native American medicine man was once asked what he thought was the most potent incantation in the spirit world. Without a second's hesitation he replied, 'It is the Lord's Prayer – the one prayer taught by Jesus Christ himself. If you Christians understood the power in that prayer you would turn the universe inside out.' The medicine man was right.

When we returned from the USA to England, we asked a group of close friends there to pray for us on a daily basis. In return, we promised to pray for them. For nearly two years, we kept these people informed of our needs – and vice versa – by post. In those long-ago days before e-mail we often couldn't afford to pay the postage for all the letters, so we often consolidated our needs into one letter which was read out in our Bible study group. Looking back now, I am certain that our letter from England read like episodes from a soap opera! Yet I am convinced that we were spared many more crushing defeats because of the faithfulness of our prayer partners.

When someone you know suffers some failure, make yourself available to pray for that person. It is especially helpful if you offer to pray *with* that person, because the human contact also may be necessary for recovery.

After I unexpectedly lost my job at a radio station in London, I was thrown off balance. One day I was a much-sought-after announcer meeting people, speaking around the country, working on fast-breaking news stories, having London by the ears six days a week! Almost overnight, my career skidded to a halt. I had no office to go to, my phone stopped ringing, and my calendar was as empty as the Millennium Dome. For a while, people wanting my services would ring me at home, but when they heard I was out of work, they never called back. Gradually, I felt that I had been yanked off the shelf and buried in the 'Past sell-by date' bin.

One day John Hine, an acquaintance from church, rang me. *Did I want to meet for prayer?* Did I? John didn't have to ask twice. We met several times at a local protestant convent that had a private prayer room. John wasn't the only one to pray with me at that time. My then pastor, Derek Walker, and an American minister named Walter Coleman, and several others, including George and Victoria Hobson, prayed with and for me. To this day, I can't be sure if it was their prayers or their willingness to spend time with me that helped me the most during a very low point in my life.

Jesus recognised the power of prayer. Consider the words of the writer of Hebrews: 'In the days of his flesh, Jesus offered up prayers and supplications, with loud cries and tears, to him who was able to save him from death, and he was heard for his godly fear' (Hebrews 5:7). Jesus said that *two* people praying is better than one: 'I also tell you this, if two of you agree down here on earth concerning anything you ask for, my father in heaven will do it for you' (Matthew 18:19, *The Living Bible*). On the eve of his crucifixion, Jesus invited his closest friends to watch and pray with him in the Garden. Although they let him down (Matthew 26:40), the principle of having prayer partners is not lost 2,000 years later.

Even if your prayers seem to be crashing into the ceiling, don't give up. Be persistent in your petition. Jesus' parables in Luke 11:5-8 and Luke 18:1-8 show us that sometimes answers to our prayers are delayed. This is never due to God's indifference, rather it is born of a love that always desires to develop and deepen a faith that is always vindicated.

For prayer to be effective, it must be expectant (Mark 11:24). We must always pray in the certainty that God will answer our petition. Beware, however. We must desire God's will, not our own, often short-sighted requests. I know a man who as a boy prayed every day that if he were to die before his parents, he wanted to be buried in his football kit. He laughs today when he tells that story, adding, 'I certainly hope no one honours that request.'

4. Don't run away from adversity

Many of us become depressed under pressure. We lose our incentive and excitement about life. Soon we escape into our own worlds to reduce emotional reactions to pain or failure.

One of the best ways to reduce the pain of failure is simply to accept it as normal. In this book, I have tried to show that it's wishful thinking to believe Christians never fail. We do. Often. But our failures needn't destroy us. Why? Because God will never abandon us. If we believe this, then each new failure may be an opportunity to grow spiritually, emotionally, and experientially. Remember, those who will not learn from past mistakes are destined to relive them!

5. Assume responsibility for your actions

The Bible says as we sow, so shall we reap. Scientists talk of cause and effect. The meaning is the same: If we are honest with ourselves and with God, then we must be willing to admit to our own mistakes. After this, we may move on, sadder but wiser. If we refuse to assume responsibility for our mistakes, we are like the young man who, found guilty of murdering his parents, stood in the dock and pleaded with the court for mercy because he was an orphan.

6. Draw upon your past failures as a means of helping others.

One of the worst failures of my life happened over two decades ago, but its effects are still with me. Judith and I had met in Bristol in October and became engaged four months later. After planning an April wedding, we flew to the USA to visit my family, who I must admit, had no prior warning that I was planning on getting married during what was to have been a year abroad as a teacher. My mother and brother were alarmed and said I was rushing things a bit. This reaction undermined my confidence regarding the suitability of our marriage.

Adding to my doubts about getting married were financial

matters. I was a low-paid teacher still paying back thousands of dollars-worth of student loans, and Judith had endured long months unemployed. Instead of joyfully anticipating the promise of intimacy, the shared pillow talk, the excitement of starting a new life with a woman that I loved, I lay awake nights worrying about facing a few years of grinding poverty followed by a divorce.

Three days before the wedding, my flatmate collared me and presented me with a fat bill for my expenses, including my share of the rates. It was well over what I had saved in the bank. This meant the little money I had planned to use for a honeymoon in the Lake District – and our first month's rent – was gone. I imagined Judith and me having no place to live. In a blind panic, I rang her parents and called off the wedding, sticking them with a huge bill for the caterer, the hall, and a hundred-and-one other costs associated with a daughter's wedding.

Several of my family and friends had flown over and were already in England before they heard the bad news. For the next three months, we were busy explaining to everyone who knew us that *yes*, we were still in love, but *no*, we weren't going to get married.

Today, I know a lot more about women – including mothers-in-law – than I did then, and I can only say I deeply regret the pain I caused my wife's family when I acted out of fear. The story isn't over though. My flatmate approached me gingerly a few days later with a new bill and admitted that he had made an error – I only owed him £56! You can imagine my anger. I was angrier still – but at myself – when our vicar casually asked why I had agonised quietly for all those weeks when he was available to counsel me.

Why didn't I speak with anyone? For most of my life, I have practised being quietly confident, preferring to suffer silently rather than bother anyone else with my problems. I see now that, in effect, my attitude was a form of pride, which in my case, preceded a very painful failure.

As I have already indicated, *no man is an island*, so for the next few weeks Judith and I sought help from professional counsellors and sympathetic, older married couples. In the end, we decided that most of our fears were imagined, and the ones based on reality were manageable with faith and hard work. So we declared our love for each other and were married in a small but terribly romantic church service miles away from Bristol.

Since then, my wife and I have had opportunities to counsel a couple having second thoughts about their engagement. We've also been able to teach about the need to put God at the centre of marriage. Of course, there are some instances when we meet people with problems too deep for lay counselling. At these times, it's wonderful to know that we may look to our church for specialist help when it is most desperately needed.

7. Don't put it off

Don't put off until tomorrow what may be done today. The time for action is *now*. If you belong to a church, go and see your minister or elders. Let them know you need help. Or perhaps you want to offer to help others in need. People's past failures enable them to draw on their experiences in order to offer sound advice to others facing similar circumstances. In any case, let people know. If you don't belong to a church, there are plenty of secular organisations that are in the business of caring.[1]

By the same author

The Church's hidden asset
Empowering the older generation

The elderly can feel just as sidelined within the Church as outside it. Yet Bible history shows that God has work for his people in every season of their lives and nobody is 'over the hill' in his eyes. Michael Apichella's heartening – and timely – review of current culture and thinking is also a resource book: a thoroughly practical guide to building creative partnerships between people of all ages for the good of the Church. MARK RUDALL

Mark Rudall is a writer and an Anglican Priest

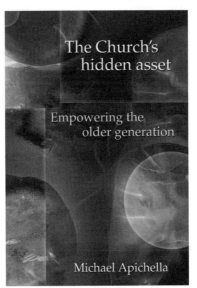

ISBN: 1 84003 701 6
Catalogue no: 1500413

If you believe that *somebody* ought to be doing something about the many problems that exist in your community, bear this epilogue in mind – with God's help, you just may be that somebody. After all, that's the answer to the question, *Why me, Lord?*

1. If you are facing an insurmountable problem and you need reliable, confidential help, don't give up. If you are lonely, depressed, hurt or grieving; or if there are issues related to pain and failure in your life that you want to talk about, I recommend the United Christian Broadcaster's Listening Line. All calls are treated in strict confidence. You may ring UCB on Monday to Friday between 9am and 10.30pm on 0870 2438787.